# THE
# RANTOUL RULES

## Dr. Steve W. Price

Published by Metaphor Press

**The Rantoul Rules**

by Dr. Steve W. Price

Copyright 2014 by Steve W. Price

Published in the United States by Metaphor Press

Metaphor Press
10427 Orange Grove Dr.
Tampa, FL 33618

The Rantoul Rules™

ISBN: 978-0-9822549-6-7

Printed in United States of America

Cover design and text layout by Parry Design Studio, Inc.

*Sometimes I think of high school as one long hazing activity. If you are tough enough to survive this, they'll let you become an adult.*

from the novel *Speak*
by Laurie Halse Anderson

# Dedication

To the senior class of 1964, Rantoul Township High School

To Dr. Rick Lyon: physician, family man,
and friend; we all miss you.

# Acknowledgment

"The values of the world we inhabit and the people we surround ourselves with have a profound effect on who we are," wrote Malcolm Gladwell in the bestselling *Outliers*.

I've been fortunate to have many wonderful people touch and steer my life over the years, beginning with my parents, Ernie and Mary Price.

When I was a sophomore in high school, Jim Wyeth, a business teacher and coach, taught me how to play tennis, which has led to thousands upon thousands of pleasurable hours on tennis courts and meeting scores of new friends, whom I would never have known if not for tennis. Here are the ones who stand out: Wes and Charlotte Brown, Bob and Maya Hardy, Greg and Hirute Harris, Jeff and Martha Wilday, Manny and Blanca Maria Velasco, Cliff Buchholz, Linda St. John, Dick Woltman, Sam Rosenbleeth, Dr. Rick Lyon, Dr. Bobby Martinez, and my wife, Carol Edler.

A long-overdue acknowledgment goes to the students I had in my classes at Southeast High School from 1968 to 1986, with a special acknowledgment to my first-hour AP English class of 1982, all of whom I remember fondly. (You're all turning 50 this year. How could that be? Seems only a few months ago you were fresh-faced 18-year-olds heading off to college.)

I acknowledge my former business partner, Burke Hedges, as the impetus for my writing books and the arbiter of how best to balance information and entertainment; and my former partner and current collaborator, Katherine Glover, for making the arrangements to get my books into the hands of readers.

And, of course, I acknowledge the support of my closest friends, most of whom I've known and revered for nearly half a century: Luke and Patti Gleason, Dave and Teri Neff, Al Taylor, Derrel Davis, Barb Bitschenhauer, the Honeyman women, Don Trello, Tim and Cathleen Shears, Kenny Price, Bill and Charmaine Smith Ladd, and Bruce and Diane Bouvier.

And finally, a tip of the hat and a hug to my extended family: daughter Sydney Price, grandson Jalen Edler, nephew Kenny Price and family, and "adopted" children Connelly and Jo Edler and Katie Edler. A long-distance hug goes to four special people in Illinois: Maya and Leah Harris, William Ladd III, and Diana Lienemann.

All of you have had a profound effect on who I am. May you all keep affecting me profoundly for, oh, another 32 healthy years, when it will be your turn to acknowledge me in my obituary. Love you all.

## School Song

*RHS, oh, RHS, faithful to you we'll be,*
*All our hopes and all our fears,*
*Will be for you just you.*
*Rah! Rah! Rah!*

*Studious days throughout each year*
*Have kept our hearts aglow.*
*We'll be loyalists and friends,*
*And until the end,*
*To the school that we love the best.*

## The only two cheers I remember

*Open up the barn door,*
*Pitch in the hay;*
*Here come the Eagles,*
*Hip, hip, hooray!*

*He's the peaches,*
*He's the cream;*
*He's the coach,*
*Of our basketball team!*
*Yay, Coach Kidd!*

# Other Books by Dr. Steve W. Price

Dream Making in a Dream-Taking World

WWW. Stands for "World Wide Whiners"

Household Gold

Surviving the Perfect Recession

How to Bounce When Others Break

How to Make Every Day Independence Day

Wrestle That Bear

# Contents

# Introduction

# We Leave High School... but High School Never Leaves Us

*In grade school I was smart but I didn't have any friends. In high school I quit being smart and I started having friends.*

—David Spade,
actor and comedian

In high school, perhaps more than any other experience in our lives, we quickly learned the difference between theory and reality.

*In theory*, we went to school to learn facts and skills that would enrich our lives and enable us to get a good job and earn enough money to live a comfortable life.

That's a nice theory. It really is.

But *in reality*, only a tiny percentage of high school students took academics seriously, studying hard and making great grades. Most of us went through the motions, doing the minimum we had to do to get the grades we needed to get without really learning much from our textbooks and teachers.

Don't get me wrong—I applaud the A students for having the good sense and maturity to take advantage of their secondary education.

I just wasn't one of them.

## My Story: Fake It 'til You Make It

In the fall of 1960, the same year Sam Cooke's ballad *Wonderful World* topped the pop music charts, I entered Rantoul Township High School. At the time, 14-year-old Steve Price had no idea Cooke's opening lyrics were a harbinger of his high school career.

Don't know much about history,
Don't know much biology.
Don't know much about a science book
Don't know much about the French I took.

No big surprise that I didn't know much about history, or any other subject for that matter. Like most high school students, I faked my way through my classes. I faked reading about Alexander the Great in World History. I faked reading about the Civil War in American History. And I faked reading the novels I was assigned in English classes. (Although years later, I read all the assigned novels and hundreds more when I was receptive to appreciating great literature.)

In high school I learned just enough—and remembered it just long enough—to do well on tests and get B grades, graduating in the top

25% of my class so that I could get into college and get on with my life.

In a word, I was a typical high school student.

## Rantoul, Back in the Day

When I was growing up in the 1950s and early '60s, Rantoul, Illinois, was like a movie set for an Andy Hardy movie: traffic-free streets on which we biked fearlessly mile after mile; a central park sprinkled with baseball fields and anchored by a gleaming municipal swimming pool; and the Home Theater movie house showing free Flash Gordon and Gene Autry movies every Saturday morning during summers.

From the first of June until the end of August, my friends and I would leave the house after breakfast and gather at the park for pickup baseball games or acrobatic climbs on the 10-foot-tall WWII cannons mounted on the three corners unoccupied by a baseball field. As we left our homes, we all received the same instructions from our moms: "Be home by six for dinner, and don't be late!"

After dinner my family would sit on the front porch, my dad in his white sleeveless tee shirt... my mom in a flowery dress with her white apron still on... my brother in beltless blue jeans, his shirt untucked, always untucked... me in my summer uniform of tee shirt, shorts and Converse Chuck Taylor All-Star basketball shoes... all of us sitting elbow-to-elbow to watch the evening thunderstorms roll in, listening to the rain drum the metal awning like a manic Gene Krupa, watching fat raindrops explode like soft wet bullets on the blacktop road and smelling the perfect smell of summer, the dizzying blend of cool rain and hot asphalt.

When night finally pulled the shades, hundreds of sleepy fireflies would float across our front yard, and my brother and I would sprint around the yard until bedtime, catching fireflies in mason jars with holes punched in the lid so they could breathe.

## The End of Innocence

For three months every summer, I was Peter Pan and my friends were The Lost Boys, playing unsupervised in our small-town-Illinois version of Never Never Land.

I'm sure Rantoul is still a great place to be a kid, to raise kids.

After all, it's populated by Heartland people with Heartland values, and these are the people and the values that built this country. But here's a tough question, an honest question: Is Rantoul as innocent today as it was when I was a kid?

Let me answer that question with another question: Today, would you let your 12-year-old child leave your home on a bike at eight o'clock in the morning and return for dinner at six o'clock with no phone calls and no text messages during their 10-hour absence? And would you allow your kid to do that all day, every day during June, July, and August, from seventh grade until their sophomore year in high school?

I wouldn't and neither would you.

Yes, our kids are still innocent, that hasn't changed.

But the world isn't innocent anymore. As the world changed, Rantoul changed along with it, and in too many ways, not for the better.

## From Farm Town to Boomtown

Here's the history of Rantoul in a thimble: Until 1917, when the War Department decided to expand the Air Force by commissioning

27 flying fields to train pilots, Rantoul was just another of the hundreds of tiny, no-stop light towns surrounded by monotonous rows of corn and bean fields downstate of the Big Bad City, Chicago. The War Department chose to build an air base adjacent to Rantoul because it was the flattest area near the Illinois Central Railroad and only 15 miles from the University of Illinois, where pilots were recruited for engagement in WWI and WWII. With the building of Chanute Field, the population exploded, transforming a tiny farm community into a bustling town. When the U.S. entered WWII in 1941, Chanute quickly became the biggest employer in Champaign County and remained so for 50 years.

My dad, Ernest Price, was stationed at Chanute when he married my mom, Mary Riley, on Christmas Eve, 1940. While in the military he taught machine shop classes, and as the war wound down in 1945, he transitioned to working for the Civil Service, first as an instructor and later as a technical writer, until his retirement in 1966.

In the 1960s, Rantoul's population peaked at 25,000, not including the 10,000 airmen who came and went at sprawling Chanute Air Force Base. The base sat at the south end of town, three square miles of barracks and landing strips and airplane hangars surrounded by a chain link fence topped with barbed wire.

The base drove the town's economy. My dad and the fathers of all my friends were either in the Air Force or worked on the base. My mom worked at a clothing store on Century Boulevard, two blocks north of the main gate to Chanute, selling over-priced flight jackets and arm patches to 19-year-old homesick airmen stationed for eight weeks to two years at the base.

## The Times, They Are A-Changin'

When I entered high school in 1960, the song topping the pop charts was *Theme to a Summer Place*, a syrupy, overly orchestrated melody written and scored for a Hollywood melodrama starring two teen idols, the hunky Troy Donahue and the perky girl-next-door Sandra Dee. Rounding out the top 10 songs were the super-sentimental *The Old Lamplighter and Teen Angel* ("What was it you were looking for, that took your life that night? They said they found my high school ring, clutched in your fingers tight.")

In the spring of 1965, my first year of college, the song topping the charts was the antithesis to *Theme to a Summer Place*, the Rolling Stones' chainsaw-electric-guitar-opened, *I Can't Get No Satisfaction* ("He's telling me more and more, about some useless information, supposed to drive my imagination..."). Six years later Don McLean's *American Pie* would look back on 1959, the year Buddy Holly died, as "The day the music died," and, indeed, with the assassination of President Kennedy in 1963, the country was in its last, lingering days of innocence.

The change in music from sentimental to cynical mirrored the changes in the country at large, and locally, mirrored the changes in Rantoul from bustling in the 1960s to busted in the 1990s. In 1988, Congress recommended slashing the bloated military budget by closing underutilized bases, which described Chanute to the letter. On September 30, 1993, Chanute was closed as a military installation and handed over to the city of Rantoul. Thousands of people lost their jobs. And the local economy lost millions of dollars.

## Rantoul Today

For two decades the city has tried its best to attract businesses to occupy dozens of abandoned buildings on Chanute's 2,200-acre site, but the efforts have largely failed. Today, the former base is home to some light manufacturing, a public golf course, and a retirement home. Officers' quarters have been converted to low-income Section 8 Housing.

But for the most part, the base resembles Detroit dropped into a cornfield.

Easily the highest and best use of the land would be to level the structures, tear up the streets, and return it to farmland. Farmland is selling for more than $10,000 an acre in Illinois today, which means the 2,200-acre plot could be worth more than $20 million. But for 75 years the Air Force had dumped thousands of gallons of fuel and untold barrels of toxic waste in on-base landfills, contaminating the soil, groundwater, and aquifer. It would likely cost more to clean up the land than a sale price could bring. So the old base sits, getting older by the day, decaying like Jimmy Webb's *MacArthur Park*, only this time it's Chanute that has been left out in the rain, "melting in the dark, all the sweet green icing flowing down."

But in the song that is today's Rantoul, the green icing is money, which has been melting out of the city for 20-plus years. In 2012, the median income in Rantoul was $32,500, $20,000 less than the median of $53,000 statewide. Little wonder, then, that the population of Rantoul has shrunk by 50%, from 25,000 at its peak in my high school years to 12,000 residents today.

Though they try, try, try, Rantoul can't get no satisfaction, either.

## The Power of a Preposition

Before we continue, I want to draw your attention to the subtitle on the cover. You likely noticed that the word "in" was marked out and replaced by the word "from." That small change in prepositions makes a big difference in the direction of this book, because for the vast majority of high school students, myself included, academic lessons took a back seat to life lessons, many of which we didn't recognize until years after graduation.

While **in** high school, most of us lacked the maturity and the emotional distance needed to extrapolate life lessons from our experiences. But after graduation, as we reflected on our high school years—the goals we accomplished... the blunders we made... the cliques we belonged to... the first loves we found... the breakups we suffered...the friends we made and lost... the jokes (and people) we laughed at... and the adolescent angst we endured—we gradually began to recognize the lessons we learned **from** high school, lessons that have stayed with us and given us a cognitive map to self discovery and helped us negotiate our way through adulthood.

## One High School, Two Educations

As I see it, we learned two types of lessons in high school—**academic lessons**, where we were taught specific lessons about a given subject, such as biology or geometry; and **accidental lessons**, where we learned general lessons about life, such as how to make new friends or how to deal with rejection.

**Academic lessons** were planned and purposeful, scripted by teachers and administrators. **Accidental lessons**, on the other hand, were spontaneous and random, usually acted out by our fellow students as if high school were a four-year group improvisation performance. Always the **accidental lessons** were exciting and tantalizing, edgy and engaging—and, yes, occasionally painful, as you'll recall, always emotionally painful and sometimes physically painful, as we struggled to discover ourselves and find our place in the social order.

From an academic standpoint, I've got more degrees than I'll ever use, so it's obvious that I value **academic lessons**. But truth be told, I came to value academics long after graduating from high school.

The lessons I learned from high school that have lasted a lifetime (and likely the ones you learned, too) happened, for the most part, outside the classroom—milling in front of the lockers before and between classes… waiting in line in the lunch room… jostling in the hallways… sneaking in quick conversations at the water fountains… riding the fan bus to ball games… slumping on gray metal folding chairs at school dances… stalling in the stairwells just before the tardy bell rings… huddling in the locker room before games… passing notes in study hall… and breaking up arguments in the student parking lot.

For me, the importance of the metallurgic tables or Hamlet's angst or learning the proof for the area of a trapezoid took a far backseat to getting a date for the homecoming dance or controlling my emotions when my cheerleader girlfriend told me she thought we should date other people. Trapezoids, shrapazoids! It killed me to see my ex giggling in front of another guy's locker. But I learned two valuable lessons from that breakup: one, the importance of maintaining my dignity in the midst of heartbreak; and two, when a girlfriend (or boyfriend) kicks you to the curb, you'll likely find an even better companion down the road.

And I did. And so did she, so the breakup was best for both of us.

That's why I say for me and the vast majority of high school students, it was the **accidental lessons**, as opposed to the **academic lessons**, that shaped our sense of self and prepared us for life after graduation.

## A Small Lesson That Changed My Life in a Big Way

When I was in Mr. Franklin's chemistry class my junior year, for example, one of the **academic lessons** was to learn the one- or two-letter symbols for the most common chemical elements.

At least, that was the theory. In reality, the only symbol I remember is gold, Au, which I have never had occasion to use since high school except for its mention in this book. Turns out that nothing I learned about chemistry has enriched my life or helped me get a job. But an **accidental lesson** I learned in Mr. Franklin's class turned out to be life altering, triggering a wellspring of passion within me and prompting my gravitating to two fulfilling careers.

First, a little back story: Mr. Franklin was a nice man and a proper man, and I'm sure early in his career he was dedicated to mentoring future Jonas Salks and Madame Curie's. But by the time I reached his class, Mr. Franklin was nearing retirement, burned out from trying to teach untalented, inattentive students like me whose sole reason for enrolling in chemistry was that it was a requirement to get into college.

Mr. Franklin wore wire-rimmed glasses and foot-wide, bold-print neckties that fell out of fashion in 1940. To fill the time and quiet us in the do-nothing days leading up to Christmas break and summer vacation, he showed films that had nothing to do with chemistry. I still vividly remember watching *The Man without a Country*, a 1937 movie about a treasonous U.S. military officer sentenced in 1807 to permanent exile aboard U.S. ships at sea without ever again seeing or hearing any mention of the United States.

As I look back, watching *The Man without a Country* struck a chord in me, keying my imagination and nurturing my nascent fascination with stories. For some indefinable reason, that movie, more than any other, contributed to my growing understanding that stories, whether in movies or music or books or Broadway plays, had powers that extended far beyond entertainment. Stories, I've come to understand, have the power to make meaning… to make connections… to take us to different worlds… to shape cultures… to reveal emotions… to predict the future… to motivate actions… to tap into our deepest fears… and, most of all, to provoke thought, to open our minds, and, on rare occasions, to change our minds.

My love for stories is why I became an English teacher, and it's why I've been writing books with lots of stories in them for 25-plus years.

## What This Book Can Do for You

Because I've been on both sides of the desk, first as a student and later as an English teacher for 16 years, I'm in a better position than the typical high school graduate to talk about the lessons we learned in high school.

Having spent 20 years in two very different high schools has given me a unique perspective on how those three or four years from ages 14 or 15 to 18 impact us for the rest of our lives. From personal experience and from many conversations with fellow classmates and former students, I've concluded that the impact of high school on our lives can be distilled into one simple sentence:

*We leave high school but high school never leaves us.*

It doesn't matter whether you rhapsodize about your high school experience, calling it the "best days of my life." Or whether you cringe when recalling those years, as was the case with movie director Steven Spielberg, who said this to an interviewer: "In high school I got smacked and kicked around. Two bloody noses. It was horrible." No matter if your recollection was pleasant or painful, we leave high school but high school never leaves us.

Some students use the momentum of the "happy days" of high school to coast into careers they seemed destined for, which describes most doctors and lawyers I know. Others take the opposite view, thinking of high school as a maximum security prison populated with sadistic inmates (the students) and run by incompetent, indifferent guards (the teachers and administrators). No matter which view best describes our years in high school, we spend the rest of our lives either trying to fulfill our potential or trying to prove the bullies and the nabobs of negativity wrong.

Either way, the lessons we learned in high school—the lessons this book identifies and reminds you about—last a lifetime. If we heed these lessons, they have the power to fulfill our potential and bring us passion, prosperity, and peace of mind.

# Every Day Is Commencement Day

---

*Glory days, well, they'll pass you by,*
*Glory days, in the wink of a young girl's eye.*
*Glory days, glory days.*

—Bruce Springsteen,
from *Born in the U.S.A.* album

---

"**D**on't peak in high school."

That was the answer I got from Nicole Davis, the daughter of a dear friend from my undergraduate days at Illinois State, when I asked what lesson she most remembered from high school.

"Don't peak in high school," she said without hesitation.

Great answer. And great advice.

Nicole certainly didn't peak in high school. By age 25 she had earned a master's degree, had worked for a year in South Africa organizing a program to identify and treat tuberculosis patients,

1

and, as I write this, is working full time in International Health and Development in Washington, D.C.

But we all know former classmates who failed to take Nicole's advice, the ones who peaked in high school: the star football player who got kicked off his college team and now, years later, bums drinks at the local tavern... the National Merit scholar who can't hold a job... the brilliant kid who got stuck in adolescence and, though in his mid-40s, is still living with his parents. Unfortunately, they all peaked at 18. For them, the next one... two... three... four decades is all downhill.

The ones who peaked in high school remind me of the caustic one-liner from comedian George Carlin, who, not surprisingly, hated high school: "Congratulations on being a cool kid in high school. Sorry about the rest of your life."

## It's Called "Commencement" for a Reason

If you've ever been to a class reunion, you'll recognize two types of people: The first group is composed of former classmates who haven't changed since high school, although they should have. You know the ones—the loudmouth... the gossip... the complainer... the bully... the druggie.

Then there's the second group, the pleasant surprises, the classmates who startle you with how much they've changed since graduation—the plain Jane who is now gorgeous... the slacker who now owns a highly successful business... the shy, quiet kid who now greets everyone with a smile and a hug and then cracks everyone up with great jokes.

The difference between the first group, whom we avoid, and the second group, whom we seek out, is growth. The ones we avoid are still mired in the past, as if frozen in time like those amber-encased ancient insects that archaeologists uncover from time to time. The new and improved group, on the other hand, embraced the future and sought out challenges that forced them to grow. They left their "glory days" behind and made new and better glory days after graduation.

The new and improved group understood the true meaning of the graduation ceremony known as "commencement," when we marched across the stage to accept our diplomas and then marched out of the auditorium to the orchestra playing the stirring *Pomp and Circumstance*. Here is *Webster's* definition of commencement:

> **Com•mence•ment: 1.** The point at which something begins, as in, "the *commencement* of the conference was delayed by an hour" **2.** The ceremonies at which degrees or diplomas are conferred at a school or college

Those graduates who thought of commencement as a beginning, as a launching pad blasting them into the orbit of adulthood, were more likely to live the lessons they learned from high school, and many went on to fulfill their dreams.

## The Lesson We Learn from Supersurvivors

The book *Supersurvivors* gets its name from a term coined by David Feldman and Daniel Kravetz to describe trauma survivors who use a personal crisis as a springboard for making huge positive leaps in their lives. "Most trauma survivors eventually recover and bounce back," the authors write. "But in some cases, they do more. They bounce forward, refocusing their energies on a new calling, a new mission, and a new path."

*Bounce forward*—isn't that a great phrase? People who bounce forward aren't satisfied with getting back to where they were before they were knocked for a loop by a trauma. Bouncing forward means exceeding the status quo, reinventing yourself, and shaping your future to accommodate your dreams.

In a very real sense, high school graduation constituted a trauma in our young lives. Of course, it doesn't compare to being diagnosed with cancer or losing a loved one. But for an 18-year-old, graduation signals that a familiar way of life—a life we'd known and understood and lived for three or four years—had come to an abrupt end. We couldn't go back to high school—that door was closed to us forever. But to us, the future looked like the real-life equivalent of the TV game show *Let's Make a Deal*. In the future, we had to choose which doors to open to "win cash or prizes," as the announcer says, but we weren't sure what was behind the door—a new car or an old goat. Which is why, I'm sure you'll recall, that the days and months after graduation was an exhilarating, but scary, time in our lives.

After commencement day, we weren't kids anymore, even though a few classmates who peaked in high school stayed stuck in the amber of adolescence, like Matthew McConaughey's character Woodson, an older guy who still associates with high school students in the classic coming-of-age movie *Dazed and Confused*. But most of us made our *commencement* into adulthood as best we could. Some landed jobs working for the city. Some went off to college. Some joined the military. Some married. Some moved. No matter what we did or where we went, we took the lessons we learned from high school with us.

## Every Day Is Commencement Day

Decades have passed since my high school commencement ceremony. But for those of us who didn't peak in high school, every day is commencement day because every day is an opportunity to begin again.

To begin reading more and watching TV less.
To begin complimenting more and criticizing less.
To begin eating more vegetables and processed foods less.
To begin saving more and spending less.
To begin daily walking and workouts.
To begin saving for retirement.
To begin a new business.
To begin becoming debt free.
To begin giving to the less fortunate.

You didn't peak in high school, so why not peak now by beginning to make yourself, and those around you, better in some way every day?

# Authority Always Wins

---

*It is not wisdom but authority that makes a law.*

—Thomas Hobbes,
17th century political philosopher

---

**I**f students get unruly in Don Trello's classroom when he's substitute teaching in one of Tampa's 15 public high schools, he calmly walks to the blackboard and writes in big letters, "AUTHORITY ALWAYS WINS!"

Invariably, a student will smirk and ask, "What's that supposed to mean?" Which gives Don the opportunity to deliver his five-minute autobiography: He worked as a prison guard for two years at Stateville Correctional Center, a maximum security prison outside Joliet, Illinois, famous for incarcerating some of the country's most vicious criminals, including mass murderers Richard Speck and John Wayne Gacy. Don followed that assignment with a 30-year career as a probation officer in Springfield, Illinois, managing and mentoring hundreds of parolees who learned the hard way that Don is right—authority always wins.

## The Lombardi Way vs. the American Way

Don Trello and legendary football coach Vince Lombardi are on the same page regarding the role of authority. A stern, no-nonsense leader, Lombardi believed his formula for success on the football field applied to virtually every endeavor in life: "Life is like football," he said. "It requires perseverance, self denial, hard work, sacrifice, dedication, and respect for authority."

Problem is, Americans have a long-standing, deep-seated distrust of authority—you could even say *disregard for authority*—dating back to the founding of this country: Referring to themselves as "separatists," Pilgrims and English Catholics escaping the authority of the Church of England settled New England and Maryland... Anabaptists rebelling against Swedish authorities and Mennonites and Amish challenging German religious authority settled Pennsylvania... and inmates from debtors' prisons in England settled Georgia.

As we all know, the United States of America was born in 1776 when the colonists declared their independence from the authority of England's King George III. Less than 100 years later, 11 southern states rebelled against the authority vested in Washington, D.C. and formed their own confederacy, leading to the Civil War. Even two legendary U.S. military leaders during WWII, Gen. MacArthur and Gen. Patton, who expected subordinates to bow to their authority, were, ironically, so contemptuous of authority that both were fired by higher-ups in the waning days of the war.

Born from rebellion and raised on individualism, American culture has long romanticized people who thumb their nose at authority—

Minutemen... mavericks... rebels... outlaws... gunslingers... non-conformists... and, yes, even gangsters. During the Great Depression, millions of destitute Americans cheered the exploits of bank robbers and murderers like Bonnie and Clyde, John Dillinger, and Baby Face Nelson, turning them into folk heroes for flouting the authorities.

## Movies Promote the Anti-Authoritarian Mindset

Movies in the 1930s and '40s, starring tough guys like Jimmy Cagney and George Raft, glamorized gangsters and prison life. Since 1930, Hollywood has released hundreds of movies set in prison, and by rewriting reality, movie studios turned common criminals and cold-blooded murderers into misunderstood victims of law enforcement's overarching authority.

For example, Robert Stroud, lionized as a gentle, self-educated ornithologist in the Academy Award-winning *The Birdman of Alcatraz*, was, in reality, a psychopath who served 54 years in prison for murdering two men, one of whom was a prison guard. And two of the highest-grossing movies in history, *The Godfather* and *The Godfather, Part II*, portray a mafia family as a legitimate business, as if they were Father and Sons Electrical Supply company instead of a murderous organized crime syndicate that made their money through robbery, extortion, and gambling.

In *The Wild One*, the classic Marlon Brando film about a motorcycle gang that terrorizes a small California town in the 1950s, Kathy, the pretty young female character working at the local general store, asks Brando's character, Johnny Strabler, "What are you rebelling against?" Johnny coolly replies, "What you got?"

Johnny's message is that rebellion is its own reward, and the coolest of the cool don't just ignore authority, they punch it in the

9

eye and pick its pocket. The seven (and counting) *The Fast and The Furious* movies about illegal street racing have grossed $2.5 billion worldwide, and the bestselling interactive video game series, *Grand Theft Auto*, has players assume the roles of three criminals, engaging in gun battles and blowing up cars in efforts to kill FBI agents.

With pop culture glorifying those kinds of anti-authoritarian messages, it should be no surprise that almost half of American males are arrested at least once by the time they turn 23, according to a study in the journal, *Crime and Delinquency*. Astonishingly, young women aren't far behind the men, with nearly 20% being arrested for non-traffic-related crimes before 23.

There are real consequences to rebelling against authority, as the young men and women who have chosen to violate the law are learning the hard way by serving time in prison. "Don't do the crime if you can't do the time; don't roll the dice if you can't pay the price," say the lyrics in the theme song for the 1975 to 1978 TV detective series *Baretta*.

## You Can Win Even When Authority Wins

There are always consequences to bucking authority, but history proves that calculated rule breaking can lead to profit making if the rule breakers have good, legal and moral reasons for thumbing their noses at authority.

For example, the founder and CEO of Apple Computer, the late Steve Jobs, hired John Scully from Pepsi in 1983 to run Apple. Jobs quickly discovered he and Scully had different visions for the company, and Jobs tried to take the company back. The board of directors sided with Scully, and in 1985, Jobs was forced out of the company he founded.

Authority won again.

But Jobs, the "loser," went on to even greater heights by reinventing himself as an entrepreneur. "The heaviness of being successful was replaced by the lightness of being a beginner again," he said years after his firing. In 1985 he founded the computer company NeXT, which Apple bought for $450 million in 1996 and then hired Jobs as CEO, where he went on to turn Apple into a hi-tech innovator with breakthrough products like the i-Pod, i-Phone, and i-Pad.

Yes, authority always wins, but, fortunately, the loser doesn't have to stay a loser. Jobs "rolled the dice" in trying to unseat CEO Scully and paid a high price by getting fired. But he used that humiliating experience to begin again with new dreams... new products... and a new business model.

## To Make or to Take—That Is the Question

If authority always wins, how do we know when it's right to challenge authority, as was the case with Steve Jobs; and when is it wrong to challenge authority, as is the case with 20-year-olds with long arrest records.

The rule of thumb is really very simple: **Taking** is bad. **Making** is good. It's bad to challenge authority if you plan to TAKE something that isn't yours... TAKE advantage of others for personal pleasure... TAKE a random risk that can hurt others... or TAKE a life unless in defense of your country or yourself. On the other hand, it's good to challenge authority if you MAKE a product or service that improves people's lives... MAKE a positive difference in the world... or MAKE something that opens doors for a new way of seeing and thinking.

In mid-19th century France, for example, the Académie des Beaux-Arts was the authority that decided what constituted "good" art. The academy determined that "good paintings" should be realistic representations of approved subjects, such as historical figures, religious themes, mythology, and portraits; and that "good paintings" were realistic representations of the subject. The more a painting looked like a photograph, the better it was, said the authorities of the day.

Then in the 1860s and '70s, along came the Impressionists, young painters who challenged the authorities. The Impressionists used brighter colors, bolder strokes, and painted street scenes, cafes, common laborers, and landscapes instead of soldiers and portraits of wealthy merchants. The Academy was appalled, but the movement caught on, and today Impressionist paintings by Cezanne, Pissarro, Manet, Monet, Renoir, and Van Gogh, among others, sell for hundreds of millions of dollars each, and over the last 150 years, the influence of the rule-breaking Impressionists has extended far beyond their paintings, transforming not only art, but also fashion, theater, movies, music, and most of all, how we think and view our world.

Steven Jobs and the Impressionists are just two examples of renegades who challenged authority to MAKE something that expands our world and changes it for the better.

# Better to Be the Employer Than the Employee

---

*The most valuable 100 people to bring into a deteriorating society would not be 100 chemists. Or politicians. Or professors. Or engineers. But rather 100 entrepreneurs.*

—Abraham H. Maslow,
psychologist

---

When people ask me what I do for a living, if I don't feel like making small talk, I'll say, "I'm a publisher." The conversation quickly turns to a different topic.

But if I want to keep the conversational ball rolling, I say, "I'm a writer." Eyes widen. Eyebrows rise. And they counter with, "Oh, I love to write. I just don't have the time." Or, "Oh, I could never write a book. I don't have the discipline or the talent." But I tell people I don't write books. What I do is write four hours a day, five days a week, and at the end of four months, a book magically appears.

When I'm writing, it's anything but glamorous. I spend lots of time wrestling with opening and closing sentences to chapters. I walk around between paragraphs, sometimes between sentences, trying to keep things clear. And interesting. And on topic.

Glamorous? No. Hard work? Not really. Frustrating work, yes. But hard? Well, compared to other jobs I've had in high school, writing is a four-month cruise on Paul Allen's 300-foot yacht.

## Detasseling Corn for $5 a Day

My first full-time employment was a six-week assignment detasseling corn during the summers after my freshman and sophomore years in high school. For you non-Midwesterners, detasseling involves pulling the yellow pollen-carrying tassels off the tops of corn stalks, allowing corn to cross-pollinate, which creates higher yields and hardier varieties. The tassels pull out easily, so it's not backbreaking work. But it is hot and sweaty work that begins at the early bird hour of 5:30 a.m., when the sun breaks orange, then yellow, over the flat green cornfields patchworked across Illinois, Iowa, Indiana, Minnesota, and Nebraska.

Back when I was detasseling in 1961 and '62, it was all done by hand. We workers would stand on 10-foot-long, two-foot-wide platforms mounted onto each side of a tractor. Two workers would stand a few feet apart on each platform. The driver would steer slowly down a middle row, allowing the workers, two on each side, to reach over a railing, pull the tassels, and toss them on the ground. The workday began wet, with dew on the corn leaves splashing onto our arms. As the sun rose, the fields dried out but the heat and humidity rose, and the edges of the leaves got sharper, snagging our gloves and whipping welts on our arms.

But we were young and broke, so we did our job, complaining little about the heat but complaining loudly when we were sent into what we called "lice fields," which were fields invaded by aphids, tiny, lice-like insects that loved munching on the tender tassels. In lice fields, the heat and humidity and boredom were upstaged by the gross factor of having to grab hard and deep at tassels crawling with aphids so your hand wouldn't slip and leave the tassel still attached to the corn stalk.

For six weeks of enduring 4:30 a.m. wakeup calls and lice fields and corn rashes and baloney sandwiches for lunch and sunburned necks, we earned 60 cents an hour, plus a 10-cent per hour bonus if we completed the entire six-week session.

I finished both sessions both summers. After taxes, I netted less than $200 each summer, which I banked for college.

## Incentive to Graduate College

Detasseling wasn't the most tedious job I had in high school.

That honor is reserved for the summer before my senior year when I spent three months building a grain elevator in Thomasboro, a farm town of 6,000 people five miles south of Rantoul.

First, some background on grain elevators: Elevators are circular, 400- to 500-foot tall structures used to store corn or soybeans. The largest elevators are built near railroad tracks so grain can be loaded onto railcars and shipped to processing plants and food makers around the country. As I recall, the diameter of the elevator I worked on was a couple hundred feet. Once the foundation was laid, workers built a wood form with a six-foot-wide trough around the circumference of the elevator. My job from 8:00 a.m. to 4:30 p.m. (with a half hour off for lunch) was to push a wheelbarrow filled with wet cement to the edge of the form and tip it forward so a guy with a flat-blade shovel could scrape it out to fill the trough to the top of the form. Then I'd walk 100 feet to the center of the elevator where the cement maker was located, get another load, and return to the perimeter, where the cement would be shoveled out and leveled inside the form.

The cement would dry overnight, and a giant hydraulic jack would raise the form a couple of feet in the morning before we arrived so that another six-foot-wide trough was waiting for me. I did this eight hours a day, seven days a week, for two and a half months, bored and blistered and burned from the sun's rays and chemicals in the cement.

As the elevator rose several feet a day (ground level when I started the job and nearing 300-feet high when I quit to return to school), I surveyed the Illinois prairie, as flat as a table top; and I surveyed the crew, half of them high school-age like me, the other half in their 30s… 40s… a few in their 50s, and I thought, "There's no way I'll be pushing wheelbarrows when I'm my dad's age."

Talk about a motivation to study in college—whenever I'd get bogged down in my studies, I'd imagine myself hundreds of feet in the air, a heartland Sisyphus, pushing a wheelbarrow to the elevator's outer edge day in and day out for eternity. It didn't take me long to get back to the books.

## Pondering My Paycheck

I don't remember complaining about the pay I received for detasseling and construction, but I do remember noticing the difference between the workers and the owners.

The farmers and seed company executives would come by their fields to check things out, and I noticed they drove late model cars and talked about grain prices and the futures' market and about increasing yields by investing in new harvesters and combines.

At the grain elevator, the owner of the construction company would visit, architectural drawings tucked under his arm. He'd meet with the supervisors. Point upward. Ask questions. Shake his head back and forth. When he returned to his Cadillac, he'd roll up his windows, even though the temperature was in the 90s, indicating his car was air- conditioned, while we laborers rolled down the windows to our dented trucks and cars.

I was only 17, and I didn't know a thing about running a business or profit margins or Profit & Loss statements. But this much I did know: It was better to be the employer than the employee. And I made a mental note that someday, someway, I'd own my own life by owning my own business.

# Prom Is Overrated

---

*Prom has all the elements of a popular story. It reeks all-Americanness, tension, drama. It has romance. Pretty dresses. Dancing. Limos. Prom, our high school coming of age.*

—Adora Svitak,
writer and public speaker

---

*I went to prom on my TV show and actually had a good time in TV world. The real world prom wasn't so much fun.*

—Nicholas Brendon,
actor

---

**I**'ve attended three proms—two proms too many as far as I'm concerned. I knew after the first one that proms were expensive, gaudy spectacles that lasted way past my bedtime.

But I kept going back for more.

My objection to proms had nothing to do with my date—I had the same date for each prom and she was wonderful. My objection was that the evening never met the expectation. How could it? My friends and I would start talking about prom months in advance... planning where we'd meet for photos... who we'd go with... where we'd eat... what songs we'd dance to... whose house we'd crash at after the dance.

So, by the time prom night actually came around and the hours piled up like discarded corsages, my cummerbund became an anaconda around my waist, tightening with each breath. Long before midnight, an existential dread would seep into my subconscious and play the refrain in the Peggy Lee song: "Is that all there is? Is that all there is, my friend?"

Yes, that's all there is. And the evening wasn't half over.

Enough already. I just wanted to sleep....

## When Prom Is Still Months Away, the Best Things Are Nearest

Okay, I'm sounding like an old fuddy-duddy. It wasn't the actual prom I objected to. It was the *anticipation* of the prom that I objected to. You see, prom only happened once a year, so the buildup to the event was so weighty—the time... the energy... the money spent on that one, singular event—that prom was bound to be anticlimactic. Same thing applies to summer vacations, seven-day cruises, trips to Paris, Christmas at the grandparents', and class reunions—they're usually a letdown because we focus so much time and attention on that one, singular event that we lose sight of the many miraculous events that occur all around us every single day.

"The best things are nearest: Breath in your nostrils, light in your eyes, flowers at your feet, duties at your hand, the path of God just before you," wrote Robert Louis Stevenson, author of the classic novel *Treasure Island.* "Then do not grasp at the stars," he continued, "but do life's plain, common work as it comes, certain that daily duties and daily bread are the sweetest things in life."

Stevenson reminds us that the lesson we learn from prom is that, to use his words, "The best things are nearest," so instead of longing after "glamorous" events that happen only once or twice a year, we should lavish our longings on the everyday, mundane things in life.

## Make Every Day Prom Night

The late Jim Valvano, former North Carolina State basketball coach, was equally passionate as Stevenson about living every day as if it were prom. His oft-quoted speech at the 1993 ESPY Awards given just weeks before he died of cancer has become a *YouTube* classic. He tells the packed audience that his daily routine hadn't changed since he was diagnosed with cancer and to live a full life, everyone should do three things without fail every single day of their lives:

"You should laugh. You should think. And you should cry. You do that, and you'll have a great day. You do those three things every day—laugh, think, cry—seven days a week, and you have yourself a heck of a life."

Go to *YouTube* and view Valvano's speech.

It puts prom into proper perspective.

# Shakespeare Still Matters

---

*Shakespeare is an international possession, transcending nations, languages, professions, and time.*

—Harold Bloom,
Yale professor and literary critic

---

T he classroom would break out with groans and within seconds a student would ask the question I'd been asked every year during my 16 years as a high school English teacher: "Why do we have to read this stuff, anyway?"

More often than not, "this stuff" was a play by William Shakespeare. After fumbling through a lame answer my first year of teaching, I decided that "Why do we have to read this stuff?" was a legitimate question, and it deserved a better answer than, "Because it's a classic," which meant less than zero to bored teenagers.

There are two very good reasons we still read Shakespeare and why he still matters—and not just in high school, but in our everyday lives: One, more than 400 years after his death, our conversations are sprinkled with dozens of catchphrases coined by Shakespeare; and two, he was the first person to blend poetry, philosophy, and psychology, giving us insights into *what* humans think and, to some degree, *how* we think.

In his 38 plays, Shakespeare fleshed out and individualized more than 100 major characters and hundreds more minor ones. Through soliloquies, the speeches where characters speak their most private thoughts to themselves and the audience, Shakespeare shows us the inner workings of his characters' minds, and by extension, he makes us aware of how we humans conduct mental debates when wrestling with moral dilemmas that don't always lend themselves to simple yes or no answers.

## Shakespeare in Conversation and Culture

Let's start our discussion of Shakespeare's relevance with a sampling of phrases from his plays that we're likely to use or hear daily, most of which we never would think to attribute to Shakespeare. Here are a few of the most common catchphrases that have endured with only slight alterations for four centuries: all that glitters is not gold... in my mind's eye... it's Greek to me... a dish fit for the gods.... there's method in his madness.... forever and a day... all's well that ends well... as good luck would have it... the world is his oyster... too much of a good thing... we have seen better days... parting is such sweet sorrow.... et tu, Brute?... the worm will turn... won't budge an inch... salad days... love is blind... this is a sorry sight... foregone conclusion... household word... one fell swoop... a comedy of errors... into thin air... and (my favorite) much ado about nothing.

These phrases are used so often they've become clichés, but on closer inspection, many of these catchphrases are packed with wisdom. For example, we've all learned, sometimes the hard way, that "all that glitters is not gold;" and we can, indeed, have "too much of a good thing." Recently, when my computer crashed, the repairman's explanation was "all Greek to me," sounding something like this: "Yadda, yadda, yadda, hard drive, yadda, yadda, yadda."

"Can you fix it?" I asked. "Yes," he replied. I was relieved we were speaking English again, and I wrote him a check for $380 without even blinking. All's well that ends well.

Not only did Shakespeare introduce dozens of pithy expressions into our language, hundreds of novelists, composers, and movie directors have borrowed Shakespeare's phrases to use as titles, including the movie and mini-series *Band of Brothers*; the novels *The Sound and the Fury*, *Dogs of War*, and *Brave New World*; and the much-quoted poem by T.S. Eliot, *The Hollow Men* ("This is the way the world ends, not with a bang but a whimper").

## Soliloquies for Every Age and Every Culture

You likely remember being assigned *Romeo and Juliet*, *Macbeth*, or *Julius Caesar* back in high school. If you were in advanced placement classes, you may have tackled *Antony and Cleopatra* or perhaps *Hamlet* or *King Lear* if you attended prep school or had an ambitious, bard-loving English teacher.

Especially in the tragedies, Shakespeare's main characters change dramatically from the beginning of the play to the end and seldom for the better. The characters develop during the course of the play because they overhear themselves speaking soliloquies, and they often respond to this inner dialogue with actions.

In Macbeth's opening soliloquy, for example, he shows his soft, caring side, singing the praises of his cousin, King Duncan, appreciating his gentleness and wisdom. Macbeth recognizes goodness and virtue in his king and further recognizes that his decision to assassinate Duncan is a horrid deed borne of Macbeth's own free will to satisfy his "vaulting ambition" to inherit the throne once the king is dead.

By the end of the play, Macbeth's soft side has been devoured by a snarling cynicism. Racked by guilt and facing imminent death, Macbeth's final soliloquy begins by describing the tedium of life: "Tomorrow, and tomorrow, and tomorrow, creeps in this petty pace from day to day," and ends with his concluding that life is short, illusory, and meaningless:

> Out, out brief candle! Life's but a walking shadow;
> A poor player that struts and frets his hour upon the stage,
> And then is heard no more: It is a tale told by an idiot,
> Full of sound and fury, signifying nothing.

Hamlet's famous "To be or not to be" speech is nearly as dark as Macbeth's soliloquy. Hamlet learns his uncle has murdered his father and married his mother, so the melancholy Hamlet questions whether or not the pain of living outweighs the joy. Hamlet is an intellectual, so he's accustomed to debating both sides of issues, which leads to his overthinking things to the point he becomes a victim of "paralysis by analysis." His very being is an internal debate that leaves him in perpetual turmoil: To act or not to act... to do or not to do... to love or not to love.

> To be, or not to be, that is the question—
> Whether 'tis nobler in the mind to suffer
> The slings and arrows of outrageous fortune,

Or to take arms against a sea of troubles,
And by opposing end them?—To die,—to sleep
No more; and by a sleep to say we end
The heartache and the thousand natural shocks
That flesh is heir to.

But Shakespeare doesn't portray Hamlet as just a one-dimensional manic-depressive. In part Hamlet is a romantic, as we learn in an earlier soliloquy, when he shows his admiration for humanity with this soaring tribute:

What a piece of work is man.
How noble in reason; how infinite
In faculty. In form and moving,
How express and nimble. In action,
How like an angel. In apprehension,
How like a god. [Man],
The beauty of the world,
The paragon of animals.

These three marvelous soliloquies, along with dozens of others, still matter because they're been read and reread, quoted and requoted, by millions of people in dozens of languages around the globe.

Why Shakespeare's durability and universality? Because Shakespeare stands alone in being both wise and entertaining. Who can challenge him as a creator of so many different selves? Who can challenge him at creating poetic and lasting phrases?

## Shakespeare: the Original Psychologist

The Czech writer Franz Kafka called literature "an ax to break up the frozen sea within us." Certainly Shakespeare was unparalleled at peering inside frozen minds of people he knew who would later become models for his many characters, breaking up the thoughts and feelings of vastly different personalities, and then writing about them in stunningly beautiful language.

Little wonder, then, that Sigmund Freud, the father of psychoanalysis, was profoundly influenced by Shakespeare's writings. Freud read his first Shakespearean play at age eight and kept Shakespeare's complete works within arm's reach for the remainder of his life. Freud's writings are liberally sprinkled with Shakespeare's character, plots, themes, and quotes as the "father of psychology" penned his theories to explain inner drives and behaviors.

If Freud is the father of psychoanalysis, then Shakespeare is the grandfather, having delved into the minds of his many characters as if he were the psychiatrist and they were his patients seeking to understand themselves.

"Without Shakespeare, we would have been very different, because we would think and feel and speak differently," writes Shakespearean scholar Harold Bloom in *Shakespeare: The Invention of the Human*.

Although dead for four centuries, Shakespeare still matters because he lives on through his insights into human nature, his language, and his literature.

Long live Shakespeare.

# Neither a Borrower nor a Lender Be

*Interest on debt works night and day, in fair weather and in foul. It gnaws at a man's substance with invisible teeth.*

—Henry Ward Beecher,
19th century New England minister

It's only fitting that a lesson about Shakespeare would be followed by a quote from his greatest play, *Hamlet*, and what better quote for a book about lessons we learned from high school than, "Neither a borrower nor a lender be."

Great advice for anyone at any age.

But at the risk of dissing Shakespeare, the quote needs an asterisk. It's a great rule in general, but there are occasions when borrowing and lending are wise strategies.

## Good Debt and Bad Debt

Let's start by talking about borrowing. I'm a big fan of Dave Ramsey, who counsels people to live debt-free. That's great advice for most consumers because the vast majority don't make a distinction between **bad debt** and **good debt**.

Knowing the difference is essential to creating wealth.

In a nutshell, *bad debt is any debt that diminishes your net worth.* People use bad debt to purchase items that depreciate in value, such as clothing, big-screen TVs, furniture, and cars or trucks.

The biggest culprit enabling bad debt is, no surprise, credit cards. According to *CreditCards.com*, there are 391 million credit card accounts in the U.S. The average credit card holder has four cards, and those cardholders who don't pay off their balances carry more than $8,000 in debt from month to month, oftentimes for years.

Credit cards deliver a double whammy on your net worth. First, they make it easy for you to buy depreciating items. When you use a credit card to buy a $100 pair of shoes, for example, as soon as you walk out the door, the shoes drop 90% in value (and that's if you're lucky enough to find someone willing to buy your once-worn shoes for $10 on eBay). Nonetheless, when your credit card statement arrives in the mail, sure enough, you're obligated to pay the full $100 you borrowed to buy those shoes. Secondly, unless you pay off the balance on your credit cards each month, you're accumulating bad debt charged at the rate of 12% to 29%. Little wonder, then, that the interest on the average unpaid balance averages more than $100 a month or $1,200 a year, further depleting the owner's net worth.

Conversely, *good debt is any debt that has the potential to increase your net worth*, such as a mortgage, business loan, or student loan. The key word in this definition is *potential*. Yeah, I know, the headlines are filled with stories about underwater mortgages and college graduates working at Starbucks while owing hundreds of thousands of dollars in student loans. But the fact remains, allowing for bad judgment, bad luck, or both, buying a good home in a good neighborhood at a good price is still a better investment than renting; and generally speaking, people with four-year college degrees earn $1.2 million dollars more over a lifetime than those with associate or high school degrees. So, yes, over time, wise investments in real estate, training and education, businesses, and the stock market pay big returns.

Robert Kiyosaki, author of the mega-bestseller *Rich Dad, Poor Dad*, sums up the difference between *diminishing wealth through bad debt* and *accumulating wealth through good debt* this way: "Rich people buy assets; poor and middleclass people buy liabilities and call them assets." That's why I say the most depressing sight in the world is a high-priced automobile parked outside a luxury apartment complex. Whoever "owns" that car and pays that exorbitant rent is diminishing their net worth by thousands of dollars each month.

Dumb, dumb, dumb!

## Further Complications

As if bad debt isn't bad enough, the middle class faces two more pressing economic challenges—incomes are going down while expenses are going up. According to the Pew Research Report, middle class income in the U.S. has fallen $3,500 since 2000, hollowing out the middle class from 61% in 1971 to 51% today. Meanwhile, expenses are going up because what the average person considered luxuries two or three decades ago are considered necessities today.

Basic "necessities" for living and working in the 21st century—smartphone service... Internet and cable TV service... and monitored burglar alarms—are costing us an extra $200 to $500 a month. Add to that $20,000-plus a year for college for the kids... increases in health insurance and drug costs... along with increases in groceries, gas prices, auto insurance, and airfares—well, no big surprise that the savings rate for the middle class is at an all-time low.

## Good Credit Means Good Debt and Good Deals Abound

As much as I deplore buying depreciating assets with borrowed money, I also recognize a good deal when I see one, and since 2009, interest rates on mortgages and consumer loans have been so low that it's foolish to pass them up.

Being fully aware that automobiles are depreciating assets, I usually buy low-priced cars with cash and keep them 10 years or more. My latest car, a Kia Sportage, is a small-size SUV that cost less than $20,000 new. I bought it mainly for the warranty, easily the best in the industry—10 years or 100,000 miles. I was prepared to write a check when the dealer told me I could get a 48-month loan for 2.25% APR. A quick calculation showed me a loan at that rate would only cost me an extra $15 a month in interest for 48 months. I jumped at the deal because it meant I could keep $20,000 in savings to use if an opportunity came my way or if interest rates should revert to the mean of 4.5% sometime in the next couple years.

I took out a similar loan on my house, which I own free and clear, to purchase a 2-bedroom, 2-bath condo in foreclosure. I borrowed $60,000 with a home equity line of credit at 2.75%. I paid cash for the unit, remodeled it, and rented it to a nice retired couple for $1,400 a month, easily generating enough cash to retire the home equity loan in five years or less. My total investment in the unit is $95,000, while the market value for similar downstairs units is $130,000 and climbing, which means I added $35,000 to my net worth during the three months it took to renovate the property.

Once the home equity loan is retired, I'll own a totally refurbished unit worth at least $130,000 located five minutes from my house in the best-located, best-maintained condo complex in North Tampa. That's what good debt can do for you—and will do for you—when you buy the right place at the right time for the right price.

## Lend to Strangers, Give to Friends and Family

Okay, time to talk about the lending side of Shakespeare's quote: "… nor a lender be." I have two rules of thumb for lending: One, don't lend money to someone if you can't afford to make them an enemy; and two, if you can't get collateral equivalent or greater in value to the loan, don't make the loan.

Rule one pretty much eliminates lending to friends and family because, let's face it, you don't want to badger a friend or family member for payment, or worse, sue them for nonpayment. Rather than loan money to friends or family, I suggest you make a one-time gift of a smaller amount. That way there's no hard feelings if things go south.

I just did that with a former student who got in a bind and needed a "loan" of $1,000 to pay her rent. "I don't loan money to friends," I told her. "But I'll give you a ONE-TIME gift of $500. No need to pay me back. You introduced me to your family, which I've been friends with for nearly 40 years, and that's payment enough." I consider the $500 "one-time gift" as insurance protecting me against any future requests from her for a loan.

As for rule two, my decision to act as a lender turned out to be the most profitable real estate deal I ever made. Here's what happened: I owned a 4-unit apartment building in a very trendy neighborhood in South Tampa two blocks from the bay. In 2006, just as the housing bubble was about to burst, a woman called me out of the blue and asked to buy my building. We settled on $365,000, with $100,000 down, and I agreed to act as the bank. I held a 5-year balloon note of $265,000 at 4% interest amortized over 30 years. She owned the property, so all I did was deposit her payment of $1,000 each month. She paid in full and on time, and at the end of five years, she owed a balance of $258,000. Because interest is collected on the front end of mortgage loans, I collected $60,000 in payments over the 60 months of the loan, but she still owed $259,000, a reduction in principle of only $6,000.

In December of 2012, I renewed the loan on similar terms, upping the interest rate to 4.5% and amortizing the loan over 20 years instead of 30. Now I deposit $1,600 a month, instead of $1,000, a 60% increase for doing the same amount of work—driving five minutes to the bank to deposit my check on the 3rd of the month.

Shakespeare should have written, "Under the right terms and conditions, it's wise, and profitable, to be BOTH a borrower and a lender."

Bad poetry, I know. But good business.

# Better a Big Bank Account Than a Cool Car

*To our surprise, we discovered that many people who live in expensive homes and drive luxury cars do not have much wealth.*

—Thomas J. Stanley,
co-author, *The Millionaire Next Door*

**M**y friends and I were really into cool cars when I was in high school. Not that we had the money to buy a cool car, mind you. But that didn't stop us from drooling over *Car and Driver* magazines.

Two cars topped our wish list in the summer of 1962 when I turned 16. My friend Paul dreamed of owning a Chevrolet Corvette convertible, like the one Tod and Buz drove around the country seeking work and adventures in the hit TV series *Route 66*. I longed for the exotic Avanti, a two-door sedan with European styling marketed as "America's only two-door personal luxury automobile."

Stylish looks and slick marketing couldn't save this poor-performing mishmash of a car cobbled together with leftover parts from Studebaker and GM. Deeply in debt, Studebaker manufactured only 4,700 Avantis; they sold poorly, and in 1963, Studebaker closed its last manufacturing plant in the States.

According to antique auto trader publications, I could buy a 1963 Avanti in mint condition for less than $25,000 today. Not sure if it would run, but it sure would look cool sitting in the driveway.

I'll pass on that purchase, thank you.

## Blessing in Disguise

The only kid in our high school with a cool car was Jimmy Joseph, a junior when I was a freshman. As I remember it, Jimmy's dad spoiled his only son, buying him a brand new Chrysler 300 for his 16th birthday. The car had angled front head lights, tail fins the size of Shamu's dorsal fin, and of all things, a spring-cushioned 45rpm record player in the trunk (I swear, I'm not making this up). Heads turned when Jimmy drove through the parking lot of the local A&W root beer stand, the front hood flowing like lava under the streetlights. We so wanted to be Jimmy.

But Jimmy sassed his dad, drove like a maniac, and by the time he graduated, the car was bent and dented, the record player long-since busted. The money for the car didn't come out of Jimmy's pocket, so what did he care?

Fortunately, my friends and I didn't have dads like Mr. Joseph. The only other fathers I knew who could afford to buy their kid a new car was Glenn Hansen, the owner of the local newspaper, the

*Rantoul Press*; and Mr. Woods, who owned the only paint store in town. Everyone else I knew lived in one-car households. It was a blessing in disguise. We were allowed to borrow the family car one night on weekends, "be home by midnight. Nothing good happens after midnight...."

I got home before midnight, no exceptions.

## Think to Invest, not Impress

At first we envied Jimmy Joseph's good fortune—in Rantoul in the 1960s, owning your own car, especially a new one, pretty much guaranteed you a good-looking date on Saturday night. But we shook our heads as Jimmy neglected his car, adding scratches and dents, burning holes in the upholstery from dropped cigarettes. We watched as the car he got for free kept dropping in value, while our small bank accounts grew from the money we earned mowing lawns for the neighbors and painting fences for the city.

At the time I didn't know anything about investing in the stock market—that would come years later. But my closest friends and I did know about investing in ourselves. We worked. We saved. We went to college. And after we graduated, we bought cars and houses with our own money and took good care of them.

As I think about the friends from high school and college that I've stayed in touch with, as well as the friends I've made since graduating, not a single one is a Jimmy Joseph, "big hat and no cattle," to borrow an old Texas saying. Of my 15 closest friends, 10 have a net worth of a million or more and the other five aren't far behind. Only two friends drive what I'd call luxury cars, which they can easily afford. And only one friend still has a mortgage, which he could pay off tomorrow if he chooses.

We've done well, I think, partly because we were lucky—the economy and stock market were booming during our peak earning years. But we also understood a lesson learned from high school: *It's better to invest than impress.*

So, we invested in education and training and careers and businesses and the stock market and real estate. But most of all, we invested in ourselves and the middle class values we learned at home and in high school: work before play… live within your means… buy for value, not status… save for rainy days and retirement… take care of your friends and family… take care of your finances… take care of yourself… and give to your church and community.

Thanks to Jimmy Joseph's lesson, I don't have a cool car. Never have, never will. But my bank account is bigger than I ever dreamed possible when I was in middle school, pedaling my bike along the black-topped side streets of Rantoul and later, when I was in high school, riding the team bus to a basketball game against the Watseka Warriors.

We were hot that night, running up 100 points on the Warriors, and we laughed all the way back home. I learned from Jimmy Joseph that it felt better to be a passenger on an aging, gear-grinding school bus celebrating a big win than to drive a new Chrysler I didn't earn.

# LESSON 8

# Life Isn't Fair

---

*The art of living is more like wrestling than dancing.*

—Marcus Aurelius,
Roman emperor and philosopher

---

**F**irst day of high school is all it took to confirm that life isn't fair.

Day one you saw cute cheerleaders (or hunky football players) who'd never go out with you... or sat in class with kids who were way-y-y smarter than you... or attended gym class with kids who were way-y-y more athletic than you... or walked the halls with kids who were way-y-y better dressed than you.

The most popular students seemed to have it all—looks, smarts, personality, confidence, clothes, and their own car in the student parking lot. And there you were, a clueless freshman with bad skin and a hall locker that wouldn't open. You didn't know where your first period classroom was and the tardy bell had just rung.

"That's not fair," you thought. And you were right.

## "That's Not Fair" Starts Young

We humans have an inborn sense that the world treats us unfairly at times. When my daughter and grandson got to the age of four, they started regularly chanting, "That's not fair," a mantra that lasts, I've discovered, until they leave the nest for good.

If I turned on the golf channel instead of a Disney movie, I'd hear "That's not fair!" If I insisted they had to eat 10 green beans to earn ice cream, I'd hear, "That's not fair!" If I told them they couldn't jump in the swimming pool until all their toys were picked up, I'd get, "That's not fair!" When I told my daughter she'd have to pay for her prom dress from her babysitting money, you guessed it, "That's not fair!" Whether it involved snacks or dinner or homework or chores or Internet access or cellphone limits, "That's not fair!" would be the response of choice. To my daughter, I was the most unfair parent in the country—until, that is, she got a full time job and started paying her own bills. (Now she tells me I let her get away with too much. Parenting—you gotta laugh.)

When we enter our teen years, "That's not fair" becomes more layered and complex, but it's still all about *me*—my looks… my place in the social order… my grades… my perceived blunders… my hurt feelings. The angst over the unfairness in high school reminds me of the refrigerator magnet I saw in a local gift shop: "You have no idea how hard it is being me."

I bought the magnet five years ago. It's still my favorite.

## Transitioning from "That's Not Fair" to "Life Isn't Fair"

When I look back on my life, I'd say I retained an egocentric view of "That's not fair to ME" through grade school, high school, and, I'm embarrassed to say, all the way through college.

It wasn't until I started teaching high school that I began expanding my worldview from myself to others. I started recognizing that life had been more than fair to me but less than fair to more than a few of my students who suffered from neglect, poverty, and dysfunctional parenting.

Gradually, my egocentric view "That's not fair to ME" was replaced by an empathetic (and more accurate) "Life isn't fair to THEM." And the older I get, the more I'm thankful for my good fortune and aware of the millions of people, perhaps billions, that life has treated unfairly.

For example, I recently received a mailer from Operation Smile, the international nonprofit agency that performs free surgeries on children with cleft palates. According to their website, 1 in 700 children in the world are born with a cleft palate.

With a world population of seven billion, that means 10 million people living today were born with a cleft palate. For them and their parents, life isn't fair. These innocent children did nothing to deserve their fate, yet the ones who survive (most die within several weeks of birth due to the inability to feed themselves) must endure taunts and ridicule for the disfigurement they inherited at birth.

The nonprofit Operation Smile is doing its best to make life fairer for victims of cleft palates. In 2013 alone, doctors with Operation Smile performed successful surgeries on 20,000 children in 63 countries. Surgery gives those 20,000 children a new lease on life. But for the millions around the globe who have no access to surgery, life will remain unfair.

## Stories of Courage and Progress

As we get older, we become ever more aware of the seemingly randomness of suffering in the world, especially when it affects children. Each year millions of innocents are born with genetic disorders, such as cystic fibrosis and muscular dystrophy; millions more struggle with neurological disorders like cerebral palsy, a permanent, nonprogressive condition that short circuits signals from the brain, causing muscles to stiffen or become slack.

What can we do to offset the seeming randomness of suffering that afflicts innocent children? The obvious answer is we can contribute to nonprofit organizations such as Operation Smile, and we can participate in events that raise money for legitimate charities. (But before you contribute, go to *CharityNavigator.org*. They review public disclosure documents to see what percentage of their donations are being spent on their missions. The American Red Cross is the embodiment of well-run charities, with 90% of its contributions going to help people in need.)

We can also improve ourselves, both personally and professionally, by abiding by the lessons we can learn from those who play the hand they were dealt with courage and determination. Jerry Traylor, for example, was born with cerebral palsy and can only walk with the aid of crutches. Yet to date, Jerry has completed 35 marathons and led an awareness campaign for the United Cerebral Palsy Association by jogging across America on crutches. The tongue-in-cheek header on his website reads, "12 people have landed on the moon. Only one has jogged across America on crutches."

Today Jerry is a bestselling author and motivational speaker whose message at hundreds of company functions is simple but powerful and speaks to every single human: "Success is learning to control our limitations, rather than let our limitations control us."

At one time or another, life has been unfair to each of us. When that happens, the best question isn't, "Why me?" That's the easy question.

As Jerry Traylor can tell you, the best question is an actionable question: "Now that life has been unfair, *what are you going to do about it?*" The right answer to that question will restore some fairness in your life and in the lives of others who love you and need you, limitations and all.

# Learn the Words to the School Song, and Sing it Loud and Often

*So be true to your school,*
*Just like you would to your girl or guy.*
*Be true to your school now,*
*Let your colors fly.*
*(Rah, rah, rah, rah, sis boom bah!)*

—Beach Boys

**T**he school song. Pep rallies. Cheers. Homecoming parades. Pride week. Letter jackets. Yearbooks. Mascots. School colors. Booster clubs. Fan buses to away games.

Today, as we look back at the events we attended and the clothes we wore aimed at encouraging school pride, it all seems so, well, "corny" is the wrong word to describe it. Perhaps "quaint," meaning "charmingly odd in an old-fashioned way," is a more accurate word.

45

Quaint? Maybe.

Necessary? Absolutely.

The purpose of the school song and all the attendant stuff was to build an organizational culture. Just as countries, corporations, tribes, teams, churches, ethnic groups, gangs, and families have cultures, so, too, do schools. To some cynics, standing at attention and singing flowery lyrics may seem like pageantry, or worse, as puffery. But because the music and the words are emblematic of the culture, school songs and national anthems are serious business.

## The Power of Cultures

Cultures contain the spoken and unspoken values and beliefs of a group or community, which in turn drive the behaviors of the members.

For example, someone who insults a member of the Mafia will likely end up dead. Someone who insults a member of the Amish will likely end up forgiven. Why two opposite reactions to the same provocation? Because starkly different cultures condone starkly different behaviors.

The converse is also true—similar cultures elicit similar behaviors. For example, the culture of Alexander Dumas' French noblemen, better known as "The Three Musketeers," is eerily similar to the culture of America's Marine Corps. "All for one and one for all," is the oft-quoted motto of The Three Musketeers; "Semper Fi," Latin for "always loyal," is the motto of the U.S. Marines, indicating that the dominant culture of the Marines is to be faithful to the corps and each of its members in peace and in war. If you were a musketeer or a Marine, rest assured someone in your group had your back. In both cultures, what was good for the group was good for the communities and the countries they served.

Unfortunately, that's not always the case. Let's take a moment to look at two vastly different corporate cultures and how they impact employees and customers.

## Portrait of a Self-Serving Culture

The first corporate culture no longer exists because the company, Stratton Oakmont, is no longer in business—and for good reason. Stratton Oakmont, a stock brokerage specializing in selling penny stocks to unsophisticated investors, was founded by Jordan Belfort, the author of the tell-all book, *The Wolf of Wall Street*, later turned into a movie starring Leonardo DiCaprio.

Stratton Oakmont specialized in a stock manipulation scam called "pump and dump." The company would buy shares of small, publicly traded stock that listed for, say, .01 cents per share. Brokers would phone novice investors and retired persons to tell them that Bill Gates was about to buy company ABC, and they needed to get in fast, as it was headed to $100 a share down the road. Once Stratton Oakmont sold 10 million shares, the stock price might rise to $1. When that happened, Stratton Oakmont would sell their 10 million shares, earning $10 million on stock they bought for $10,000. Shortly after Stratton Oakmont dumped their shares, the stock price would plunge and thousands of naïve investors would be left holding worthless stocks.

The corporate culture established by the founder, Jordan Belfort, was to sacrifice all scruples at the altar of money. Because the corporate culture taught that money was all that mattered, brokers were encouraged to lie and deceive in order to accumulate more money so they could buy faster cars and bigger boats and throw bigger drug-fueled parties.

No big surprise, their corporate symbol was a pirate flag.

By the time the brokerage was shut down in 1995, it had swindled investors out of $200 million; the founder and CEO, "the Wolf of Wall Street," was convicted of stock manipulation and sentenced to 22 months in prison.

## Portrait of a Servant Culture

Contrast the culture of Stratton Oakmont, the ultimate self-serving culture devoted only to themselves and the almighty dollar, with the servant culture of Hobby Lobby, a privately owned, debt-free company with 500 retail craft stores in 41 states. Below is the Hobby Lobby Statement of Purpose from their corporate website:

> *In order to effectively serve our owners, employees, and customers, the Board of Directors is committed to:*
>
> *Honoring the Lord in all we do by operating the company consistent with Biblical principles.*
>
> *Offering our customers an exceptional selection and value.*
>
> *Serving our employees and their families by establishing a work environment and company policies that build character, strengthen individuals, and nurture families.*
>
> *Providing a return on the owners' investment, sharing the Lord's blessings with our employees, and investing in our community.*
>
> *We believe that it is by God's grace and provision that Hobby Lobby has endured. He has been faithful in the past, and we trust Him for our future.*

Hobby Lobby backs up their statement of purpose with actions. They pay their employees above-average salaries for the industry, and although they take in a billion in sales annually, they keep their stores closed on Sundays, potentially their most profitable day, costing the company $100 million in lost revenue.

When you look at the contrast in cultures between Stratton Oakmont and Hobby Lobby, it proves that learning the words to the school song and singing it loud and often is more than just a meaningless pregame tradition—it's a commitment to shared values and beliefs.

"If you don't stand for something, you'll fall for anything," goes the old saw. And it's true. Organizational cultures set the tone and direction for the actions of everyone in the group, and if you don't or can't subscribe to the culture, then you need to remove yourself from the group and join a group that is more aligned to your values and beliefs. No one forced employees to stay with Stratton Oakmont. And I'm sure some people resigned when they refused to condone their corrupt culture.

Same goes for employees and customers of Hobby Lobby. I'm sure a few of the 16,000 employees have left for other jobs because they couldn't abide the conservative Christian culture. And I'm sure some consumers refuse to shop at Hobby Lobby because the background music in all the stores is solely Christian music. That's fine with Hobby Lobby's founder and CEO, David Green, his family, and his board of directors, for their culture has served God and themselves well for nearly half a century.

## A Purpose-Driven Business

When Green and his wife started his business in 1970 making miniature picture frames in their garage, they decided to base their

49

family business on Biblical principles. Knowing they couldn't please both God and every, single consumer, the Greens sided with God. As David Green says in his bestselling book, *More Than a Hobby: How a $600 Startup Became America's Home and Craft Superstore*, "Seek to please God in everything you do. Run your business in harmony with God's laws. This will keep you on ethical footing."

Whether you agree or disagree with David Green's philosophy, all I know is this: If Jordan Belfort had adopted the culture of Hobby Lobby when he founded Stratton Oakmont, he wouldn't have gone to prison and his company would still be in existence and likely flourishing.

As you have seen, cultures can make a huge difference in how people run their businesses and live their lives.

So choose your cultures carefully—and then stand and sing the school song loud and clear and often. Rah, rah, rah!

# Seek Extra Credit Every Chance You Get

*There are no traffic jams along the extra mile.*

—Roger Staubach,
NFL Hall of Fame quarterback

I define a "dear friend" as someone you might not talk to for years, decades even, and when you finally get together, you start your conversation in mid-sentence, as if one of you just returned to a lively dinner conversation after a short bathroom break.

That's the kind of friendship Steve Larkin and I have. Recently Steve visited me in Tampa for a few days. We hadn't seen each other in nearly 30 years, but our teasing and laughing began the moment we hugged hello at the front door and lasted until we hugged goodbye the next afternoon as he departed for his flight back to his home in Huntsville, Texas.

I first met Steve my junior year in high school. His dad, a career military man, had been transferred to Chanute Air Force Base in Rantoul. Some kids have trouble fitting in at new schools. Not Steve. He was athletic and funny and a bit rebellious, so the guys liked him. And he was movie star handsome, so the girls gushed over him.

I can't remember the details of how we became friends, but I do know this: If we met on, say, a Friday afternoon, by Friday evening we both knew we were dear friends.

## Extra Credit Post High School

In late July 2014, Steve made the 40-minute drive to my house in Tampa from Thonotosassa, a small working-class town known for its fish camps and barbecue joints, where he had attended the funeral for the father of another dear friend of his.

Steve was only spending one night with us, so he didn't have much luggage. He strolled toward his room, a carry-on bag in one hand and a bouquet in the other. "What's with the flowers? I asked. "For your bride," he drawled. "Nice of you, but you didn't have to do that," I said, although I was impressed by his thoughtfulness.

"I didn't fall off a snap pea truck," he smiled as he set the arrangement on the kitchen counter. "This is the least I could do for a woman I've never met who opens her home to me."

I *expected* Steve to bring a bottle of wine as a courtesy. I expected Steve to offer to pay for dinner. But a colorful bouquet for my wife? That I didn't expect and neither did Carol, which made it all the more special.

Steve's unexpected gift was the adult equivalent of earning extra credit in high school—and he definitely received extra credit from

Carol when she was greeted by flowers from a stranger when she got home.

## Why Extra Credit Was Extra Important in High School

You remember extra credit in school, don't you? By doing extra math problems or writing extra book reports, you could raise your grade, sometimes a little, sometimes a lot.

I was a B student in high school, so anytime there was an extra credit assignment, I jumped on it. I figured I needed all the grade inflation I could get. But what amazed me is the number of students who blew off extra credit. Guess they figured it just wasn't worth it to spend an extra few hours on homework to raise a B+ to an A-.

They were wrong.

Because extra credit wasn't a requirement, you weren't punished if you didn't do it. But you weren't rewarded if you didn't do it, either, and the reward far exceeded the effort. Back in high school, you didn't impress teachers when you handed in an assignment on time. You were expected to hand in your assignments on time.

But students who did extra credit impressed teachers because it showed them you had initiative. It showed teachers you were willing to take the extra step. It showed teachers you weren't content with making an average effort. It showed teachers you listened to them. In a word, it showed teachers they mattered and that you cared about grades... about school... about yourself... and about them.

That's lots of "showing" for a little effort, wouldn't you agree?

And that's why you should seek extra credit whenever you can, for as long as you can, whether you're an 18-year-old senior or an 88-year-old senior citizen.

## Why Extra Credit Makes Everyone Feel Better

"You didn't have to do that," my wife kept saying to Steve, as she admired the bouquet.

And she was right. He didn't have to do that. But that's what earning extra credit after high school is all about—making memorable moments by going a step or two beyond expectations.

I once heard a speaker make an astute observation: "Most people will forget what you say. Some will forget what you do. *But no one will ever forget how you made them feel.*" The lesson we learn from high school about earning extra credit is that doing the little, unexpected things for people makes them feel good... makes them feel respected... makes them feel listened to... makes them feel honored... makes them feel appreciated... makes them feel special... makes them feel loved.

## Turning Her Back on Extra Credit

Back to Steve's overnight visit. His flight didn't leave Tampa until 7:00 p.m., so I had time to show him the sights in Tampa. Just after lunch I drove us to Tampa's historic district, Ybor (pronounced EE-BORE) City, named after the founder, Vicente Ybor, a Spanish-born cigar manufacturer.

In 1884 Ybor bought 40 acres of scrubland northeast of Tampa and built not just cigar factories but hundreds of two-bedroom 600-square-foot houses for his immigrant workers from Cuba, Spain, Italy, and Germany, which they could buy interest free by deducting

$1.50 per week from their wages. As a result, the population of Ybor City exploded from a few hundred in 1886 to 6,000 four years later. At its peak in the Roaring Twenties, Ybor City was the cigar capital of the world, producing 500 million cigars annually.

After taking Steve on a brief tour of the 10-square-block historic district, I pulled into Don Vicente de Ybor, a two-story boutique hotel that served as a hospital from 1926 until 1968; it remained abandoned for 30 years before being renovated and converted to a 16-room hotel in 1999. With its wrought-iron balconies and pink-stucco façade, the building was certainly charming. But Steve and I immediately spotted weeds in the parking lot and sidewalk, and it was obvious the four potted ficus trees guarding the entrance hadn't been watered in days.

"If they don't take care of details on the outside," I said to Steve, "I hate to think how often they launder the sheets." Steve nodded and said, "Little details indicate big things in hotels and restaurants. No way would I stay in this place. No way."

When we entered the lobby, our criticism gave way to awe, as we marveled at the 40-foot ceiling, the winding staircase, and the wood-paneled walls. We made small talk with the only employee, a cute college-age woman behind the front desk. After a self-guided tour, we returned to the front desk. The woman looked up from her iPad, answered a few of our questions, and then smiled and waved goodbye as we made our way across the 100-year-old hardwood floor. Steve walked over to a potted ficus tree, dug his fingers into the soil, and shaking his head, muttered, "Soil is dry as a bone." They'll die if they don't get water soon."

I tell this story as an example of people who turn their backs on extra credit. The lobby was empty when Steve and I entered, so the woman at the front desk had ample time during her shift to grab a pitcher and water the potted plants. But she didn't. Why? Because she wasn't expected to water plants. Her job was to greet and register guests. Watering plants was someone else's job, so it never got done.

Obviously the Don Vicente de Ybor, and the woman who worked there, didn't have a culture that encouraged and rewarded extra credit. Not hard to figure out why the place was empty, is it?

## Same City, Different Story

Steve and I concluded our tour of Ybor with a stop at the Ybor City Museum, a converted brick bakery adjoined by six restored "casitas" built for cigar workers. As we entered a courtyard next to the museum, Steve spotted a giant vine snaking 20-plus feet up an old oak tree at the rear fence.

"Look at those leaves," he barked. "They're the size of elephant ears. I bet I could grow those on our property in Texas. What's the name of that vine?" he asked me. I hadn't the faintest idea. But Steve was on a mission, so once we were inside the museum, he asked Brian, a park ranger, the name of the vine. Brian didn't know either, so he asked Brenda, the other ranger on duty.

"Don't know, but maybe I can find it in here," Brenda said as she made a beeline for a storage room, where she dug out a binder of tropical plants and sat with Steve thumbing the pages in search of the unknown vine. No luck. By this time, the two rangers joined Steve on the mission to track down the name of the mystery vine. They brainstormed names of people who might know the plant's name. They made phone calls. They searched websites. Thirty minutes later, after Brian gave Steve and me a personal tour of a refurbished casita, their detective work paid off.

"It's called a Devil's vine," Brian announced. "It's a common indoor vine but can be grown outdoors under the right conditions." Steve typed a note in his smartphone and headed outdoors to take a photo to show to his wife. When I see Steve in six weeks at our upcoming high school reunion, you can bet I'll ask him where he planted his Devil's vine and how it's doing.

## Moral of the Story

Within six blocks and an hour's time, Steve and I witnessed the opposite ends on the extra-credit scale.

We were equally appalled at the neglect at the Don Vicente Hotel. It was like someone owning a 1956 Ferrari sports car and never washing it or changing the oil. It's worse than neglectful—it's shameful.

And we were both amazed at the rangers' enthusiasm and their eagerness to go out of their way to answer a visitor's question. Next time an out-of-town friend stops by for a visit, the museum will be at the top of my must-see places.

Our tour of Ybor City reminded Steve and me that a little extra credit goes a long way and that little things are big things when it comes to buildings. And restaurants. And museums. And careers. And relationships. And whatever else you can think of.

Meeting someone's expectations is nothing special. Expectations are just the baseline, just the average, just ordinary.

No one raves about ordinary.

No one keeps coming back for more ordinary.

But people will keep coming back for more *extra*-ordinary.

The surest way to turn the ordinary into the *extra*ordinary is to seek extra credit every chance you get.

# You Never Stop Getting Graded

---

*There are advantages to being elected President.*
*The day after I was elected, I had my high school*
*grades classified Top Secret.*

—Ronald Reagan,
40th U.S. President

---

In the county just north of Tampa, the poisonous cloud of political correctness has seeped into the office of the Pasco County Superintendent of Schools.

On July 1, 2014, led by the urging of Superintendent Kurt Browning, the school board voted to eliminate the valedictorian and salutatorian designations, replacing them with Latin designations *cum laude*, meaning with honor, to recognize more students with high grades.

"I believe there is a better way to recognize the highest achievers," Superintendent Browning told *The Tampa Tribune*. Seems that

Browning wants to eliminate the practice of recognizing only two students per year "...to encourage more students to strive for excellence."

Using Superintendent Browning's line of reasoning, The Masters Golf Tournament should eliminate the champion and runner-up designations and recognize all 96 golfers invited to the tournament so that they would all strive for excellence (which, obviously, 94 of the 96 do not do), with the added bonus of no one getting his feelings hurt.

If there is "a better way to recognize the highest achievers," why stop at high school or golf? Let's eliminate the Most Valuable Player award for all sports teams... let's eliminate the head coach of football teams... and, while we're at it, let's eliminate the title "Superintendent of Schools" and replace it with the Latin designation, *cum communism*, to encourage more employees to strive for the collectivist ideal.

## Let's Get Real about Grades

Okay, okay, I got a bit carried away there. But in case you didn't get my point, let's extend Superintendent Browning's reasoning to its logical conclusion: To make sure that ALL students strive for excellence, schools should simply eliminate giving grades (which reward the highest achievers while punishing less talented students or those who don't study or turn in assignments). That way every student would automatically skyrocket to the highest achiever status overnight.

Problem solved—until, that is, all these nongraded students graduate from Fairy Dust High School and enter the real world, where they will be graded every day in every way for the rest of their lives.

Look, I was a teacher, so I know the argument against giving grades: Low grades hurt self esteem… grades are culturally biased… grades don't really reflect how much a student has learned… grades are oversimplifications of the complex learning process… "easy" teachers might give 90% of the students A's and B's, while "hard" teachers in the same subject might give 90% C's and D's… blah, blah, blah.

Hey, there's some merit to each of those objections, but the ultimate, overriding argument in favor of grading comes down to this: We're all graded every day in every way in everything we do, so we might as well get used to it. For example, most companies have some kind of "annual review" whereby the managers or bosses sit down with their subordinates and evaluate their strengths and weaknesses as "excellent, satisfactory, needs improvement, and on probation." To me, work evaluations sound the same as grades A, B, C, and D, with F standing for "fired."

## The GE Way: Get Good Grades or Say Goodbye

Jack Welch, the legendary CEO of General Electric, introduced the 20/70/10 system for ranking employees: The top 20% were deemed the most productive and rewarded with raises and promotions; 70% of employees were rated "adequate" and encouraged to improve; and the bottom 10% were classified as nonproducers and fired. Welch applied a variation of the same system to his top executives, ranking them as A, B, or C. He fired C executives, encouraged B executives to leverage their strengths and improve their weaknesses, and rewarded A executives with bonuses, promotions, and stock options.

Employees derisively called Welch's evaluation program the "Rank-and-Yank System," but from a productivity standpoint, it worked. Under Welch's leadership, GE had a 28-fold increase in earnings from 1981 to 2001.

## Grading Used in Professional Sports

To some people, Jack Welch's Rank-and-Yank program may seem cold and callous, but professional athletes understand how harshly their work is judged—and how profoundly it affects their paychecks. After every practice and football game, NFL coaches "break down tape," meaning they evaluate videos of every play, grading each players A through F. Only the A and B players remain on the team after training camp and preseason games are finished. The C and D performers are cut and told to clean out their lockers. Old and injured players, no matter how popular they are with the fans or teammates, are shown the door if they can't perform at the highest level.

Other sports have their unique system for grading athletes. Baseball has four skill levels: Single A, the lowest, Double A, Triple A, and the Major Leagues. To get to the Majors, players have to excel at each level, moving up until they get the call to join the Big Leagues. And once there, they have to keep performing at the A or B level or they're demoted to a farm team or "released," a professional sports euphemism for "fired."

The ATP lists the top-ranking 100 players and the PGA gives the top 125 players a touring card each year. Top golfers on the many tours scattered around the globe can easily earn $200,000 to $300,000 a year, and the top 10 PGA players earn millions. Players who drop out of the rankings due to poor play or injuries must play their way back to the top of the rankings or take jobs as teaching pros at a country club.

Same goes for professional tennis players. Every time they play a match, they receive a pass/fail grade—they pass when they win, fail when they lose. Players who pile up failing grades to low-ranked players don't get invited to play in tournaments. No tournaments means no income, so it doesn't take long for unranked players to pack up and go home. In every professional sport, players either "make the grade" by winning, or they flunk out of school, so to speak.

If some people think poor grades in high school hurt self-esteem, how do they think aging tennis players or injured golfers feel about themselves when the tour no longer wants their services? Must be devastating, especially for the hundreds and hundreds of low-ranked players who don't earn enough money to save for the day when their phone stops ringing.

## Judging Just Another Word for Grading

Think of all the TV shows that use judges as part of their format: dance competition shows... singing competition shows... talent shows... there are even business competition shows, such as *The Apprentice*, where Donald Trump fires a different contestant at the end of each episode.

In effect, the judges are grading the contestants before millions of viewers: Comments range anywhere from an A ("That was brilliant") to an F ("That was awful"). On many of these competitions, the TV audience acts as the judge by voting for their favorite performers.

And over the years, there have been dozens of shows featuring real judges handing down real legal decisions, such as *The People's Court* and *Judge Judy*. Make no mistake, the participants on these shows are being graded. The judge delivers a pass/fail based on the testimony and credibility of the plaintiffs and defendants. Personally, I find these shows cringe worthy—hard to find anything to like about fatuous defendants and arrogant judges. But the fact that the shows remain on the air indicates that viewers are giving the shows a passing grade, for ratings are everything when it comes to TV.

The only medium that exceeds TV in giving grades is the Internet. *TripAdvisor.com* allows travelers to grade hotels, restaurants, and airlines. *Amazon.com* encourages readers to grade books and products. And *Angieslist.com* empowers consumers to grade local companies and services. With the Internet, ordinary people are empowered to release their inner high school teacher and "grade" doctors and dentists and restaurants and appliances and movies and about anything else you can think of.

Admit it—it feels pretty good to be the giver of grades, doesn't it?

## Me?... Judgmental?... Guilty as Charged!

"Don't judge me," became one of my daughter's favorite expressions when she returned home for the summer after her freshman year in college.

No question I was judging her that summer. I judged the color of her hair, which she had dyed midnight black, as not as flattering as her natural brunette. I judged her half-inch false eyelashes to be a bit over the top. (My first thought was they looked "camelesque," but I wisely kept that comment to myself.) And I judged her room to rival the Fukushima nuclear disaster.

So, yeah, I was judging her. And so does everyone else who sees my daughter. I read in *Psychology Today* that it only take seven seconds for us to evaluate someone we meet for the first time. In those seven seconds, our minds do thousands of calculations assessing looks, attitude, intelligence, body language, confidence, status, and so on. In a very real sense, you're being flash graded on a laundry list of qualities and attributes.

What's really scary is that these first impressions are usually accurate and nearly impossible to reverse or undo. "You never get a second chance to make a first impression," goes the old saying. So true. And so important to our happiness and success.

When you think about it, dating is an agreement between two people to grade each other. If each of you rates the other an A or B on the first date, there will likely be a second.

So, to those people (my daughter included) who say, "Don't judge me," I say, "Get real, 'cause you're gonna get judged—you're gonna get graded—all day, every day, in every way." Telling people not to judge you is like telling them not to breathe. Judging, breathing, eating—they're all essential to human survival. Our cave-dwelling ancestors learned to make accurate snap judgments because it was often a matter of life or death, and we inherited that valuable skill from them. If a village sentry, for example, mistakenly judged an approaching stranger as a friendly wayfarer when he was really an enemy scout, the entire village could be wiped out. Quick judgments were, and still are, essential to our health, wealth, and happiness.

## Sometimes We're the Judge, Sometimes We're the Jury

A better question to ask in today's world is, "Who are you to judge me?" If your boss or your spouse or your pastor is judging you, I suggest you listen. If they're consistently giving you C's and D's and the occasional F on your conduct, you need to change your behavior.

Keep in mind, however, that not everyone's judgment is equally valid. If, for example, an avowed atheist judges you, calling you a "superstitious Goody Two Shoes," well, that might be the best unintended compliment you'll ever receive; likewise, if the broke, nasty, negative neighbor judges your new business venture as, "One of those things that never works," consider the source.

In both cases, THEY are the judges. But never forget, YOU are the jury. And when all the evidence is heard, it's the jury that delivers the final decision.

# Homework Never Ends

One of life's most painful moments comes when we
must admit that we didn't do our homework, that we
are not prepared.

—Merlin Olsen,
NFL Hall of Fame lineman

**T**om Peters, the author of *In Search of Excellence*, one of the
best-selling business books in history, liked to tell the story about
when he first recognized that preparation for success is a lifelong
pursuit.

As a 17-year-old junior in high school, Peters' girlfriend invited
him over for a Sunday dinner at her home. Her father was a successful
surgeon, and they lived in a lovely house overlooking the ocean. After
dinner the family gathered in the living room to talk. Just minutes
after everyone settled in, the father excused himself and retired to his
home office, where he read the latest medical journals and reviewed

procedures for the operation he was scheduled to perform the next morning.

Peters remembers thinking that it wasn't fair that a middle-aged doctor with 10 years of education after high school—four years in college, three in medical school and three more as an intern—should still have to do homework.

"It just didn't seem fair," Peters wrote, "that homework would never end."

Until this incident, young Peters assumed you went to school to get filled up with all the knowledge you'd need for the rest of your life, and after graduation, you wouldn't need to study or do homework ever again. He was shocked... SHOCKED...to learn otherwise.

## Better Late Than Never

Successful people understand that homework never ends until, well, life ends. (Unsuccessful people don't understand this, which is one big reason they're—you guessed it—unsuccessful.)

Frankly, I didn't learn that homework never ends until my 40s. All through high school, college and much of my 16-year teaching career, I winged it, doing just enough preparation to do a respectable job. Until I was 40 years old, I had A+ potential but did a C- job in my work because I was lousy at preparation.

Let's just say I was nonchalant when it came to homework.

That changed when I went into business for myself. I quickly discovered that to book new business, I couldn't settle for being as good as the competition—*I had to be better than the competition.* So, to survive in business, I had to ratchet up all phases of my game, and that meant spending more time on my homework, taking more pride in my preparations. The better I got at my homework, the better

I got at my jobs... which led to my getting more jobs... which led to making more money... which led to my getting more opportunities.

By the time I'd reached my fifth year in business, my commitment to preparation evolved from nonchalant to obsessive. Today, I over-prepare for writing projects. I read three newspapers daily and subscribe to a dozen magazines. I research projects for four to six months... organize the material... write multiple drafts... check the facts... do an oral read-through with an assistant... proofread the copy... check the printer's proof... and then print a short run to give to clients for their feedback.

Is all that homework worth it? You bet! I get to set my own hours, choose my own projects, and work out of a home office. Beats detasseling corn and pushing wheelbarrows of cement around the top of a grain elevator, wouldn't you agree?

## From Terror to Tutorial

Because of my renewed commitment to homework, I discovered three valuable lessons while preparing for a speech in Seattle, Washington, on my book *Household Gold*. I hadn't given a talk to a more than 30 students in one of my English classes since 1986, so when I agreed in the fall of 2005 to give a 50-minute talk to 1,000 people in a hotel ballroom, well, let's just say I was more than scared.

I was terrified.

I didn't get a full night's sleep for the three months leading up to the speech. I tossed and turned. I paced the floor. I dreamed about going blank halfway into my speech. So, there was no way I was going to be nonchalant with my preparation. In fact, I went overboard on my preparation: I wrote the speech and highlighted the key words and phrases. I rehearsed my speech standing behind a podium I constructed from a discarded cardboard box I snagged from the rear of an appliance store. I rehearsed my speech in front of the sliding mirror doors in my wife's closet. I rehearsed my speech in the morning in my pajamas, in the afternoon in a suit, and in the nighttime in my bed. And from all that rehearsal, I discovered three rules that are the keys to peak performance:

1. Know your material
2. Know your audience
3. Know yourself

It doesn't matter whether you're giving a speech or performing surgery, if you master these three rules, you'll have a great outcome. Let's take a brief look at how to get the most out of each of these.

## 1. Know Your Material

"The man who does not read is no better off than the man who cannot read," said Mark Twain. So read daily... read diligently... and read widely. Obviously, you need to read in your field so that you know your product, know your industry, and know your craft. But don't stop there. Read tangentially—personal growth books, business books, news magazine, *National Geographic*, arts and crafts periodicals, *Architectural Digest*, whatever, because you never know when an article or a photograph or a cartoon will resonate with you and open doors to new insights into your business and your life. The opening story for one of my books came from a marketing brochure a guy handed to me in an airport. Instead of tossing the brochure in the trash, I read it and discovered a brief story about an old violinist that was perfect for the book I was working on at the time. So read, read, read.

Also, get information and instruction whenever you can: Attend live conferences and trainings, watch webinars, go to meetings, seek mentors, ask questions, talk to leaders, seek out successful peers—that's how you gain know-how, knowledge, and wisdom.

## 2. Know Your Audience

The audience for my speech in Seattle was predominantly aspiring entrepreneurs. Which meant most had jobs but were looking for more money or more control or more freedom in their lives. I didn't want to load them down with facts and statistics. I wanted to inspire them and tell them the benefits of being your own boss and the essence of what makes a great opportunity. I knew that even if they took notes, they wouldn't remember more than a few things I said, so I limited my talk to five key points and anchored those points with visuals and stories they would remember. I closed the speech with a story about my dad, a recovered alcoholic who remained drink-free for the final 20 years of his life. When I ended my story, I saw a few teary faces in the front row, so I knew I touched the audience, which validates the quote in Lesson 10 about what people remember: "Most people will forget what you say. Some will forget what you do. But *no one will forget how you made them feel.*" So, know your audience. Know their dreams, their hopes, their fears. Know what moves them. When you touch an audience's feelings, you'll touch them for the rest of their lives.

## 3. Know Yourself

When I was preparing for my first speech, I attended five or six live seminars to see great speakers in action. One speaker really stood out. He spoke without notes for more than an hour. He rushed from one side of the stage to the other, telling stories, making jokes, asking questions. At one point he went down on one knee, like the legendary performer Al Jolson singing *Swanee*. One moment he would raise his voice and flap his arms wildly. The next moment he would whisper so softly the audience would have to lean forward to hear him.

71

When his speech ended, he had to towel off in the wings, and the audience cheered and stomped until he returned for a curtain call. His performance was brilliant, and it reminded me that I had my work cut out for me because, frankly, I could never deliver a performance like that. Ranting and raving and commanding the stage like Mick Jagger of the Rolling Stones—well, I knew myself well enough to know that just isn't my style. To try to imitate that performance would be laughable, embarrassing even.

So I decided to be myself, to work with my strengths while compensating for my weaknesses. My strengths were these: I had great information that my audience needed to hear and some bittersweet stories about growing up with an alcoholic dad and my years as a teacher. My biggest weakness is that I'm easily distracted and have a lousy memory, so I needed lots of notes to help me get through my presentation. No way was I going to read a speech for 50 minutes and put 1,000 people to sleep. So I devised a way to keep myself on track while keeping the audience interested.

## Show and Tell

Although my speech was about my book *Household Gold*, I opened by telling the audience I had been a teacher for 16 years, and "once a teacher, always a teacher," which allowed me to structure the speech as a "show and tell." I lifted up five props for the audience to see—a sign for a garage sale, a Walmart flyer, a bottle stopper, a heart made from construction paper, and an audio tape recorded in 1974. Using props meant I was able to give five, 10-minute speeches instead of one 50-minute speech, which was much less taxing on my memory and much more interesting for the audience.

As I ended my speech, my voice cracked as I talked about my father's battle with alcoholism and his eventual triumph over addiction, remaining drink-free for the last 20 years of his life. When I finished, the audience jumped to their feet, and I received high fives and hugs from the organizers as I made my way backstage.

I wasn't best speaker to ever appear before a live audience. I don't have any illusions about that. *But I was the best speaker I could be*, because I did my homework.

But I didn't settle for just *doing* my homework. Truth is, I *labored* over my homework.

And it paid big dividends for me, just as it can for you.

# Procrastination: Harmful in High School, Deadly in Adulthood

*One of these days is none of these days.*

—Old English proverb

My dad and I have something in common—we both had an ongoing battle with a bad habit.

His bad habit was alcohol.

My bad habit was procrastination.

Under the right circumstances, they're both life threatening. Don't get me wrong—I'm not trying to diminish the disease of alcoholism. I'm merely trying to emphasize the seriousness of procrastination. Too much procrastination can be just as deadly to your physical and financial health as too much drink.

## My Struggle with Procrastination

As I mentioned earlier, I was an indifferent student in high school and my early years in college. I never studied for a test or wrote a report until the night before it was due. But two episodes in my college years cured me of procrastination.

The first happened in my junior year at Illinois State. One of my courses, the History of Western Civilization, was a requirement for graduation. At the time, I thought history was boring. To complicate matters, I didn't like the instructor. So, after the first lecture, I stopped going to class. The night before the final I cracked open the textbook for the first time, figuring I'd stay up all night and learn just enough to pass the final.

Talk about naïve—this was the entire history of Western civilization, from the ancient Greeks and their city states to the founding of the United States. The textbook was easily 400 pages long. I got to page 12 and fell asleep until the alarm rang at 7:00 a.m. for my 8:00 a.m. test.

I failed the final and failed the course. Didn't get a single answer correct.

Talk about a wake-up call! I had never failed a class before. And for some airheaded reason, I thought I could bluff my way through this one. I was wrong, and I learned a valuable lesson: I didn't like the feeling I got seeing an F on my report card. It was insulting. It was demeaning. It was humiliating. I didn't like being labeled a "failure," and it motivated me to be more diligent in my studies. I retook the class the following semester. I never missed a lecture, read every assignment from cover to cover, and earned a B. And for the first time, I actually enjoyed learning about history.

That was lesson one that led to my recovery from procrastination.

## Writing My Dissertation

Lesson two happened 15 years later as I was finishing up my doctorate. I had completed my coursework and passed my comprehensive exams. All I had to do to finish my degree was write my dissertation, which is like saying all Christopher Columbus had to do to discover America was sail across the Atlantic Ocean.

A dissertation is a lengthy, written document on a specific subject in your field of study. Mine, with the clunky title, *A Synthesis of Materials for Using the Process Approach to Teaching Professional Writing*, was 177 pages, double-spaced on 8½ x 11 typing paper.

In all honesty, my dissertation was pretty lame. But it got me the degree I was seeking, and that's better than 50% of the people who finish their coursework for a doctorate but never get around to writing their dissertation. You see, there's a three-letter acronym used in doctoral programs to describe students who finish all the requirements but their dissertation. The acronym is "ABD," and it stands for "All But Dissertation." Being ABD is like running a 26-mile marathon and then dropping out with only 100 yards to go. I mean, why spend three to five years of your life and tens of thousands of dollars only to quit with the finish line in sight?

Truth be told, if it weren't for a phone call in the spring of 1985, I could easily have been ABD, because I'd fallen off the procrastination wagon. I was reading books, taking notes, making outlines, interviewing professors, but I wasn't doing the one thing I needed to do to earn my degree—I hadn't started the arduous task of sitting down and writing my dissertation. Then one afternoon in April I called Ray Wallace, a 25-year-old fellow classmate from Northern

Ireland, to ask him how he was coming on his dissertation. For me, that phone call was literally a wake-up call.

"I'm done," he said. "Finished it and defended it two weeks ago. You can now call me Dr. Wallace," he teased.

After I hung up the phone, I stared at my computer, which I hadn't even bothered to turn on. Ray Wallace, a guy 16 years younger than me, had completed his dissertation while I hadn't even started mine. My competitive nature kicked in, and my reignited pride shoved my procrastination out the window. No way was I going to be ABD when a friend in the same program had finished his.

I started writing that afternoon, finished the dissertation in three months, and was awarded my doctorate on August 10, 1985. In May 1986, I resigned from my teaching job and that October I loaded up a U-Haul truck in the rain and steered onto I-55 South, heading for Tampa, Florida, to start a business owned and operated by Dr. Steve W. Price.

Dr. Ray Wallace, wherever you are, thank you, thank you, thank you.

## Why Procrastination Is Deadly

I define procrastination as "a mental agreement between your wants and your willpower to avoid one ounce of pain in the present in exchange for 10 pounds of pain in the future."

Procrastinate eating vegetables in your 20s, and you could have diabetes in your 40s.

Procrastinate exercising in your 30s, and you could have a heart attack in your 50s.

Procrastinate saving for retirement during your working career, and you could end up broke in your 60s.

Procrastinate getting a colonoscopy, and you could die of a very curable cancer.

This isn't just scare tactics—research proves that procrastination can be deadly. Let's take a few moments to examine how procrastination can decimate us financially and physically.

## Millions Unprepared for Retirement

Here's a scary statistic from a report by the Federal Reserve Board: Nearly one-third of Americans have no retirement savings or pension, including 20% of those ages 55 to 64. Worse yet, nearly half adults aren't even thinking about planning for retirement.

I've heard the excuses: "We don't have any money left at the end of the month to save for retirement." Really? The average family has enough money to afford big-screen TVs... enough money to pay for premium cable packages... enough money to take the family on a cruise... enough money to buy smartphones for everyone in the family.

But not enough money to save for retirement? Get real.

I call this phenomenon "procrastination by priority." The millions of people who are putting off saving for retirement aren't putting off buying stuff that gives them immediate gratification. Why? Because for most people, pleasure in the moment takes priority over the pleasure of being financially free in retirement.

If people don't make saving for retirement a priority... if people don't make losing that extra 50 pounds you gained since high school a priority, then it will get put off until some future date that never materializes.

Then one day they'll wake up, and they're 60, and mandatory retirement for their job is 65. And they wonder how they'll pay for food, pay the rent, and pay off the $6,000 in credit card debt they carry from month-to-month when their only income is Social Security.

## Losing Weight Can't Wait

The only thing scarier than being broke in retirement is being sick and broke in retirement. And frankly, America (and increasingly the rest of the world) is eating itself sick. Seven out of 10 Americans are overweight, and 35% of Americans are classified as obese.

Little wonder, then, why 40% of Americans born between 2000 and 2011 will develop diabetes. As I write this, 30 million people in the U.S. have diabetes. The majority of those have type 2, which typically develops in adults and is linked to a sedentary lifestyle.

So, the question becomes, "If 70% of Americans need to lose weight to avoid everyday aches and pains and the onset of diabetes, when are they going to push away the pizza and start exercising regularly? Answer: AFTER the holidays... AFTER the kids leave home... AFTER I turn 40... AFTER whatever, AFTER whenever.

But that day never comes until the blood work comes back positive for type 2 diabetes or until the heart attack or stroke hits like a lightening bolt.

That's why I say procrastination is harmful in high school— maybe you got a C on the big test in biology instead of a B because you put off studying until the night before. That's harmful.

But diabetes. And heart attacks. And strokes. They can be deadly. The sad thing is, in most cases, they're avoidable. So remember, losing weight can't wait. Neither can regular exercise.

Here are three numbers that can get you back to your ideal weight:

3,800 — average calories Americans consume each day

2,600 — calories nutritionists recommend each day

2,000 — number of steps it takes to walk a mile; doctors recommend 10,000 steps a day, five days a week

No more procrastinating! Commit to getting that top number of 3,800 down to 2,600 by eating less processed food and more fish, fruit, and vegetables. And set a goal to take 10,000 steps every day.

Oh, and no more tomorrows. No more excuses. Get started today!

# Don't Let Others Define You... Define Yourself!

*Don't let the noise of others' opinions drown out your own inner voice.*

—Steve Jobs,
commencement address at Stanford University

I want to share two very different stories about the importance of defining yourself.

The first story is close to my heart—it's about my daughter, Sydney. The second story is close to Tampa, where I live. It's about Harris Rosen, a hugely successful hotel owner and operator in Orlando, Florida, less than an hour's drive from my home.

Let's begin with Sydney. When Syd was a high school junior, she started hanging out with two students who were, let's just say, unhealthy influences. As was the case with most 17-year-olds, Syd desperately wanted to be liked. She was more of a follower than a leader back then, so if a popular, charismatic student took an interest in her, Syd would glom onto him or her.

In this case, it was "him" *and* "her," two classmates who were brazen, unconventional, and self-assured, three things Syd was not but desperately wanted to be. So she became their acolyte. Problem was, they weren't interested in accepting Sydney for who she was. They were interested in molding her into a carbon copy of themselves— brazen, sullen, defiant, snotty, self-absorbed teenagers.

## The Body Snatchers Invade High School

Before continuing my story about Sydney and her struggles to define herself, first I need to fill you in with a brief backstory. Living with Sydney during her junior year in high school was like living in a scene from the classic sci-fi movie, *Invasion of the Body Snatchers*. By all outward appearances, my daughter looked like the same Sydney, but aliens had hijacked her demeanor and personality

I first saw the horror movie *Invasion of the Body Snatchers* with a group of guy friends when I was 12 years old. We whooped and hollered throughout the movie, pretending we weren't scared. But it terrified me and is the reason I won't watch horror movies today.

The movie was based on a 1955 science fiction novel and has been remade twice by Hollywood since the original 1956 black-and-white version I saw. The plot is classic sci-fi horror: Intergalactic pods drift down from outer space and land on a military base in California. The three-foot-long pods are really aliens in the form of giant seeds that morph into physical duplicates of humans while they sleep. Once the pod's transformation to human likeness is complete, the sleeping humans turn to dust.

The scariest part is that the characters in the movie and the audience couldn't tell an alien pod-person from a human, so the good guys couldn't be distinguished from the bad guys, which created a compounding sense of paranoia on the screen and in the theater. The subtext of the movie was right out of the *Communist Manifesto*: Individuality was the cause of the world's problems and only conformity could save the world. (The film captured the paranoia of the times, when in 1954 Sen. Joseph McCarthy told Congress he had ferreted out 205 communist spies in the State Department.)

There was an obvious parallel between the body snatchers in the movie and the two high school students who were seeking to remake my daughter in their image. They wanted to "podify" her, keeping her outward appearance but transforming her into a fellow alien.

It was up to her mom and me to become "Ghostbusters" and break the hold the body snatchers had on our daughter.

## Sent Away to Boarding School

We sent Sydney to a therapeutic wilderness program in North Carolina for two months, followed by a year at Oakley, a therapeutic boarding high school in the Wasatch Mountains 20 miles from Park City, Utah.

Sending Syd away for her senior year was the toughest decision I ever made but the best one. The year away broke the bond with her devious "friends," and after graduation from Oakley in the fall of 2009, Syd enrolled in college in Salt Lake City, where she has lived ever since. Today she works full time in the city and has made many new friends who aren't interested in transforming her but accept her the way she is—pretty, smiling, saucy, lively, and loving. She's defining herself in a healthful, natural way and surrounding herself with like-minded friends.

Can you tell I'm proud of my daughter? Let me add, deservedly so.

## Respect the Mouse or Move On

The second story begins in early 1970, when a Disney employee named Harris Rosen left California for Orlando to help in the final stages of construction of Disney World, just south of Orlando.

By his own account, Harris loved working for Disney, but the Disney hierarchy didn't return the love. Seems that Harris was a bit too independent for their liking, and in 1973, despite exceeding all his goals, Harris was fired. In his exit interview, the powers-that-be commended him for doing a great job, but they told him they were letting him go because, in their words, "He most likely would never become a fully integrated Disney person." He further alienated the superiors by sarcastically asking, "So I'm being terminated because my ears are too small?"

"Harris, that is the kind of negative attitude we are talking about," said a senior manager. "It has become obvious to us that you don't really respect the Mouse, so today will be your last day."

So, 34-year-old Harris was fired for not respecting a mouse. "That day it became apparent to me that if I was going to be happy and fulfilled, I had to be in business for myself."

That was the day Harris defined himself as an entrepreneur. Within months he bought a 256-room Quality Inn. He put down everything he had in his bank account, $20,000, and assumed a mortgage of $2.5 million. After the closing, he went into his new office, put his head on his desk, and cried, thinking he had done the dumbest thing in his life. But he did have a plan to increase the occupancy from a piddling

15% to nearly full occupancy by offering rock-bottom rates, living at the hotel, and doing a host of jobs himself, saving almost $250,000 a year.

One year later, he bought another 250-unit hotel on International Drive. He was on his way to building a small dynasty. Today Harris owns seven hotels and resorts adjacent to Disney totaling 6,400 rooms.

## Never Stop Defining Yourself

Harris not only defined himself financially in his 40s, but he also defined himself physically, starting a daily routine of swimming a mile each morning and eating only healthy foods (he consumes an average of six ounces of salmon daily).

At the age of 55, Harris made another huge leap in defining himself. By then he owned five hotels and was planning a sixth and dreaming of a seventh, "when it suddenly became clear that it was time to start giving back."

He donated 20 acres and $10 million to the University of Central Florida in Orlando to build a College of Hospitality Management. That same year he created an education and scholarship program for Tangelo Park, a high-crime neighborhood, where his foundation provides free preschool education for every child in the neighborhood. He proudly points out that the Tangelo Park elementary school has been rated an A school by FCAT for eight consecutive years. Harris' foundation also offers fully paid scholarships, including tuition, room and board, and books, for every child in Tangelo Park who graduates from high school and is accepted to college. To date, more than 200 high school graduates are attending college and 100 have already graduated.

## A Cautionary Tale about Following Others

My daughter, a 23-year-old just starting out in life, and Harris Rosen, 75-years-young, have both learned why it's not just important, but essential, that you define yourself.

I was once again reminded of this when I read about three Japanese tourists in Australia who mechanically followed the GPS system in their rental car straight into the Pacific Ocean. They set their destination as North Stradbroke Island on the Australian coast. As they drove along, the GPS guided them from a paved road to a gravel road into a muddy road leading into the bay at low tide. The GPS map failed to show the nine miles of water and mud between the mainland and the island.

"It told us we could drive down there," Yuzu Noda told the local newspaper. "It kept saying it would navigate us to a road. There was lots of mud." Noda and her friends drove about 50 yards into the bay when they realized they were hopelessly stuck. As the tide began to rise, they abandoned the car and waded back to shore.

This true-life story serves as a parable for people who follow others blindly instead of listening to their own voice and defining their own course in life. Whether its chasing away body snatchers… disrespecting a mouse… or overriding a faulty GPS… the lesson is clear: To discover your true path in life, define yourself. Otherwise you'll get bogged down in someone else's mud.

# Worst Yearbook Advice: "Don't Ever Change"

---

*There is only one corner of the universe you can be certain of improving and that is your own self.*

—Aldous Huxley,
British author

---

"**D**on't ever change!"

Five different classmates wrote that statement in the yearbook for my senior year: "Don't ever change."

Good thing I didn't take their advice, or I'd still be living in Rantoul in a 900-square-foot home with my parents, driving a 1956 Studebaker stick shift, and cruising through the parking lot of the A&W root beer stand on Friday night looking for girls to ask out for Saturday night.

Not a good life plan, do you think?

That's not to say I don't know some people who took the "Don't ever change" advice to heart. Tim, a guy I knew who didn't change, was large, loud, profane, obnoxious, and impulsive in high school. He's still all those things today and is now serving seven years in a minimum security prison in Vandalia, Illinois, for embezzling half a million dollars from a family trust.

Actually, he did change. He changed for the worse—to my knowledge, he never stole in high school.

## National Merit in High School to No Merit as an Adult

In the end, we all have a choice about change. We can change for the better, like most of us do. Or we can change for the worse. This lesson you're reading is about changing for the better, of course.

But before we talk about the strategies people use to change for the better, I want to tell one more story about someone who changed for the worse, because her life exemplifies what NOT to do to grow personally and professionally after high school.

Deborah attended an all-girls Catholic high school in the city where I was teaching. I knew of her because tennis buddies of mine said she had the whole package—smart, pretty, and personable. Did I say smart? She was super smart, a National Merit Scholar. From the more than 3 million high school seniors, only 8,400 are awarded the distinction of National Merit Scholar. Bill Gates, founder of Microsoft, was a National Merit Scholar. So was Jeff Bezos, CEO of Amazon.com.

That's very select company.

After college, Deborah graduated from law school. She returned to Springfield, the state capital, where she could work for either a private firm or state government. Only 25 years old, she took a job with the justice department. Her future was full of promise. One problem—Deborah hadn't made positive changes in her life since graduating high school. Because she had such a high I.Q., she hadn't developed her E.Q., that is, the ability to manage emotional states in yourself and others. People with a high E.Q. exhibit discipline, grit, perseverance, and resilience, which empower them to succeed in the face of hardships and adversity.

Because school came easy for Deborah, she didn't have to work hard to get good grades. So she never developed good work habits. She procrastinated. She was poorly organized. She made excuses for being late to work... made excuses for shoddy work... made excuses for a bad attitude... and made excuses for missing deadlines. She finally missed one deadline too many, allowing a hardened criminal to go free because her legal brief missed the judge's deadline. That was the final straw. Less than a year after being hired by the justice department, her superiors gave her a choice: resign or be fired. She resigned.

## Fired but Not Fired Up

Being fired is devastating. I know that. I was fired twice, and, frankly, I deserved it both times. But post-firing, I did something that Deborah didn't do. I did some soul searching. I sat down by myself and analyzed the reasons I was fired. And during that sit-down, I made the honest assessment that I needed to make some changes if I was to become successful in business.

I needed to find jobs that played to my strengths. I needed to be more conscientious about my work. I needed to deliver not just *on* deadline, but *before* the due date. I needed better preparation. And I needed to do more than meet the clients' expectations, I needed to EXCEED expectations.

My firings were a long-overdue wake-up call for me. I'm proud to say I woke up, went to work, and was richly rewarded for the positive changes I made in my life.

Deborah did the opposite. After her forced resignation, instead of having a heart-to-heart talk with herself, she threw the pity party of all pity parties—she blamed her boss... blamed the job... blamed society... blamed the state government... blamed the federal government... blamed everyone but herself. Her pity party has lasted more than 20 years and is still in full force. She moved back home ostensibly to take care of her aging mother, who was in failing health but certainly able to live by herself. Deborah received wages from her mother for grocery shopping, cleaning, and the like until her mother passed away.

Once Deborah was no longer needed as a caregiver, she was free to go back to work. But she didn't. And still hasn't. Instead, she remains in her childhood home, burning through a small family inheritance. Meanwhile, the neighborhood is deteriorating around her... the house is deteriorating around her... and her life is deteriorating around her.

What a waste of God-given talent, all because she wouldn't take personal inventory of herself and make changes that would make her a better lawyer, a better citizen, and a better person.

## To Change, Tour Your Junkyard

Toyota is always at the top of the ratings for quality and reliability.

It didn't happen by accident. I read recently that Toyota regularly has its engineers tour junkyards to examine Toyota wrecks. They learn lots with these tours: Which parts rust most easily. Which sections hold up well in collisions. The engineers were looking for that kind of thing. But on their tours, something popped up they weren't looking for. They discovered that the side mirrors were often broken off, even on later-model cars that hadn't been in bad accidents. So the engineers designed fold-in mirrors, which have become standard on most new cars.

The point of the story is this: Toyota sells more cars and makes more profit than any other automobile manufacturer. Why? Because they take inventory. They turn the camera inward. They assess themselves as thoroughly as the consumers and the competition.

Sometimes we need to do the same. We need to take an objective tour of the junkyard of our lives to assess what we've done right and need to do more of, and what we've done wrong and need to improve on. I know, I know, we'd all rather go to an awards banquet than tour a junkyard. But awards banquets are for what we accomplished in the past. Junkyard tours are for what we can do better in the future. That's why successful people abide by Yogi Berra's unintentionally humorous insight: "I don't live in the past. There's no future in it."

## Failure Is the Best Teacher

In the book *How Children Succeed*, author Paul Tough argues that schools need to focus more on personal skills and less on cognitive skills. He thinks "grit, curiosity, and the Hidden Power of Character" are the ultimate keys to success in school, sports, and life.

"There's just this increasing body of evidence and awareness about how traits such as resilience, zest, optimism, self-discipline, and conscientiousness affect success. And I've noticed that business people caught on sooner than academics or educators that these character strengths really matter... and these skills really do matter in quantifiable ways in child development, in education, and in the workplace," writes Tough.

Failure, I've learned, is not a death sentence unless you choose to make it so. "Failure is an opportunity to begin again, this time more intelligently," said Henry Ford. That was certainly true in my case, but not in Deborah's case. Instead of choosing to get better, she chose to get bitter. The opposite ways she and I chose to respond after having suffered the same indignity of being fired (and in my case, not once but twice) has made a 180-degree difference in the arc of our lives.

The irony is, she's still the smarter than I am. She'd still outperform me by 20 points on an I.Q. test. But she hasn't changed in positive ways since high school. I have. And that's made all the difference.

## Bouncing Back from the Ash Heap of Failure

When I started this chapter, I didn't intend to write so much about failure. But the more I reviewed my research, and the more I thought about making positive changes in life, the more I realized that it's failures that force us to make detours on the road of life.

Without failure, there's no reason to change our behavior, is there? But when we experience a failed relationship... a failed presentation... a failed proposal... a failed product... a failed dinner party... a failed investment... a failed anything—those are the occasions that prompt successful people to make purposeful, positive changes.

The business world is populated by hugely successful people who bounced back from firings and failures. When Bernie Marcus was fired from a chain of hardware stores at age 49, he had few options. So he did what he had been talking about for years: He started his own hardware chain. Two years after the first store opened, his chain was doing so well that Marcus and his partners decided to take the company public. If you had bought $1,000 worth of that stock in 1980, you'd be rich today. The name of the company is The Home Depot.

Here's another story of a failure turned billionaire. James Dyson, founder of Dyson vacuum cleaners, created a vacuum that used centrifugal force to separate dust and dirt, so there was no need for a bag. For three years he pitched his product from one vacuum manufacturer to another, hoping to land a licensing agreement. No takers. Hamilton Beach, Black and Decker, Eureka, Kirby, and Electrolux all said a vacuum without a bag wouldn't sell.

After 5,000 prototypes and a long list of rejections, he finally understood that if he wanted to make his dream come true, he'd have to manufacture it himself. When he launched his first vacuum in 1993, it became the number-one-selling vacuum in 18 months. Ten years later he was a billionaire.

## Fail Better

Avant-garde playwright and novelist Samuel Beckett wrote the anthem of every entrepreneur who overcame failures and adversity to achieve success: "Ever tried. Ever failed. No matter. Try again. Fail again. Fail better."

That's what James Dyson did—he failed better. Each prototype he came out with improved on the previous one. Each proposal he gave to giant manufacturers improved on the previous one. But to no avail. He kept failing better until he failed his way to becoming a billionaire.

Failing better. Learning from mistakes. Turning adversity into advantage. That's what successful people do. The others quit and move back home.

You can fail better, or you can quit.

Which do you choose?